DAVID H

ASK, BELIEVE, RECEIVE

7 Days to Increased Wealth,
Better Relationships, and a Life You Love
(...Even When it Seems Impossible)

ASK, BELIEVE, RECEIVE

7 Days to Increased Wealth,
Better Relationships,
and a Life You Love
(...Even When it Seems Impossible)

by
David Hooper

For more information on this series, please visit us on the web at
BoldThoughts.com.

ISBN: 978-0975436196

KRE, LLC
PO Box 121135
Nashville, TN 37212-1135

CONTENTS

HOW TO ATTRACT YOUR BEST HEALTH

HOW TO ATTRACT YOUR DREAM JOB

HOW TO ATTRACT EVERYTHING NEEDED FOR A SUCCESSFUL BUSINESS

How I Discovered the Law of Attraction...

I was first exposed to the "Law of Attraction" when I was in high school. I had just turned 16 and my friend's grandfather gave me a copy of *As a Man Thinketh* by James Allen.

A few years later, while looking through the used book section of a local "new age" store, I found some old recordings by Earl Nightingale. Being in the music industry, I was aware of Earl Nightingale, since he was the first person to have a spoken word album achieve Gold Record status (500,000 copies sold) with his *Strangest Secret* album.

Coincidence? No.

Working within the industry, with bands and musicians of all levels of success, from "garage" acts to those playing arenas, and seeing firsthand that the one major difference in these acts wasn't musical talent, but the level of "success mindset," I started to put everything together...

Soon, I started to write about the subject.

When the film *The Secret* was released in 2006, I was in the right place, at the right time, with the right material. And soon a new aspect of my career was born...

Coincidence? No.

The Secret exposed the world to the Law of Attraction in ways James Allen, Earl Nightingale, and others hadn't. It reached millions of people, many who would never set foot in a metaphysical bookstore or New Thought church.

It was a very good start. Unfortunately, with all the discussion surrounding the Law of Attraction – from Oprah, to Larry King, to the *New York Times* – there was a lot of misinformation and people quickly became confused as how to best use it.

I originally wrote this book as a supplement to material such as *The Secret*, in order to help people get a true understanding of how the Law of Attraction works, from personally working with it in their lives, rather than just reading about it. It's a step-by-step formula, actually five of them, to help you achieve what you want in specific areas of your life – money, relationships, health, employment, and business. Each is divided into seven steps, so you can complete it in one week.

This book is about simplifying the Law of Attraction into an easy-to-follow, step-by-step procedure, that anybody can follow. Simply follow the steps and take things one day at a time.

Since the original version of this book was released in 2008, I've received feedback from thousands of people who have been impacted by its teachings. It has been very gratifying to think that what started out as a personal interest has reached so many people.

Of course, in additional to the great feedback I've received,

I've also gotten a lot of questions. This edition of the book answers some of the most pressing ones.

Whether you're new to the Law of Attraction, or like me, read everything you can about it, I hope you'll find the step-by-step plans within this book beneficial in helping you to manifest the life you desire.

If you have any questions, or would like to connect with other like-minded people to discuss the Law of Attraction, I hope you'll drop by my Web site at BoldThoughts.com. There, you'll find more information on the subject of Law of Attraction as well as audio interviews with Law of Attraction experts and other related material.

Thank you!

David Hooper
Nashville, TN

PS – As a bonus for reading this book, I'd like to give you a free audio book of another title I've written, *The Rich Switch*. This book focuses on how you can achieve more wealth in all its forms and you can download the audio version right now, at RichSwitch.com, as my gift to you.

INTRODUCTION

Whether you are brand new to Law of Attraction principles, you've been having a hard time getting it to work in your own life, or you simply want to take these principles to the next level, this book is going to lead you through a simple process for mastering these life-changing techniques.

Using the Law of Attraction in a deliberate manner is actually very simple to do, but our confused thoughts can often create a great deal of uncertainty, doubt, and disbelief. As a result, our negative thoughts get in our way and prevent our desires from becoming physical reality.

I won't promise that the information in this book will make you an instant millionaire or make all of your dreams come true in the blink of an eye. For the majority of people, the larger manifestations will take a bit of time to develop.

Once you experience even small results from using these techniques, however, you're going to be impressed enough to continue working with them and to eventually go on to become a dynamic attractor!

What is the Law of Attraction?

The Law of Attraction is activated by your thoughts, beliefs, and emotions. In short, whatever you think about and focus on the most, you'll tend to attract into your life.

What do you think about most of the time? Are you usually

in a good mood or a bad mood? Do you feel hopeful and optimistic about the future, or do you experience a lot of fear and anxiety about your circumstances?

According to the Law of Attraction, you will attract situations and events that match your thoughts and feelings. Most often, the principles of the Law of Attraction should not be taken as a literal representation. For example, you wouldn't attract a giant spider just by thinking about one. And you probably won't attract a great deal of money by simply hoping for a million dollars.

Think of the Law of Attraction process in more general terms that are based on the corresponding frequency of vibration you send out to the universe. If you experience a lot of frustration and anxiety, you'll probably attract plenty of situations that keep inciting those feelings in your circumstances (job problems, money problems, relationship problems, and so on). Likewise, if you experience a lot of joy and satisfaction in your life, you'll probably keep attracting more situations about which you can be happy.

For the majority of people, the entire Law of Attraction process takes place on a subconscious level. Since they don't realize the power of their thoughts and emotions, they attract many things and situations by default – some good, some bad.

When you decide to start consciously working with the Law of Attraction, however, you can greatly increase the occurrence of good experiences and reduce the amount of "bad" experiences.

Don't think of the Law of Attraction as a magical cure for life's little issues, as using these techniques doesn't mean you'll never experience problems again. You'll still have challenges to overcome, goals to meet, and rude people to deal with now and then. You'll probably still have days where you feel a bit down or stressed. It's life! The Law of Attraction won't enclose you in a cushy cocoon so you never have to deal with problems again – but it can give you greater control over how many of those problems you experience.

Changing your life with the Law of Attraction is more about gaining control of the quality of most of your experiences by awakening to your true power as a deliberate creator. Once you fully grasp the techniques and become confident in using them, you'll be empowered to shift your life in the direction you want – while having the power and self-assurance to deal with problems and challenges if, and when, they occur.

In addition to your frequency of vibration, your beliefs play a large role in what you will allow into your life. Even if you're sending out the frequency needed to attract something you want, a belief that you don't deserve the change or that it's impossible to attain will be enough to block it from arriving.

We'll be exploring the power of your beliefs a bit later. But, for now, just know that you'll need to take a close look at any beliefs that may be preventing you from achieving your life goals.

Understand also that the Law of Attraction is completely impersonal. It doesn't reward or punish you – it simply gives you what you ask for (even if you're not aware that you're asking). According to your thoughts, beliefs, and emotional frequency, you bring forth whatever is in alignment with you.

Many people, upon learning about the Law of Attraction, attempt to persuade or even trick the universe into giving them what they want. They believe that if they say the right words, visualize the right things, and do everything just right, the universe will swing open the gates of prosperity and deliver their deepest desires. Likewise, these same people fear that by wording something the wrong way or not focusing on the right things, the universe will punish them by withholding the things they want. There are no punishments or rewards, except those that *you* decide on. What you emit, you attract.

Putting the Law of Attraction to Use

In the following chapters, you will find specific instruction on how to use the Law of Attraction in *every* area of your life. Each week you will learn how to look at the things you most value and learn how you can attract more of what you want and less of what you don't.

Follow the daily exercises, taking one element of your life at a time to really focus on what it is that you want in this area. By taking time each day to become more aware of what you are creating (and what thoughts are keeping you from having everything you want), you will be able to fully integrate the Law of Attraction into your life in a way that works for you.

To help you with the process, I encourage you to keep a journal of any thoughts, ideas, affirmations or "ah ha!" moments that come to mind as you read through each daily exercise. Be sure to check out my Web site **BoldThoughts.com**, for a place to share your experiences with others.

I wrote this book with the hope that it will help you to live the life you've always dreamed of.

Good luck in your journey!

How to Attract Money Into Your Life

Day 1 – What is the Law of Attraction and How Does it Affect Me Financially?

You're probably used to thinking of money as a tangible object that resides in your wallet and bank account until you're ready to use it. You pay bills with it, purchase products and services with it, and maybe even donate some of it to worthwhile charities.

Where does this money come from? If you're like most people, you probably have a job or business through which you exchange time, products or services for money. This is the most common way to receive money, but did you know you can also attract it with the Law of Attraction?

Have you ever wondered why some people have a lot of money and others have so little? You may be tempted to say that the former group must work hard and the latter group doesn't, but that's not always true, is it? There are plenty of people who work very hard but still barely manage to make ends meet each month. There are also plenty of people who don't work at all, yet have millions of dollars in the bank.

Assuming both groups have the same potential for opportunities, the difference between them is usually a little something called *mindset*.

One group has a wealth mindset, while the other group has a lack mindset. The Law of Attraction is activated by your mindset, which is determined by all the things you think and feel on a regular basis.

Here's how it works: Your thoughts trigger your emotions. Your emotional state emits a specific frequency of energy to the universe. In turn, the universe returns events and experiences into your life that correspond with your emotional frequency.

When you think and feel positively on a regular basis, everything in your life seems to flow more easily, including money. On the other hand, when your thoughts and emotions lean more toward the negative side on a regular basis, you experience more problems, setbacks and financial lack.

Also important are your beliefs, as they form the structure of what is possible for you. If you believe you have to work hard to have a lot of money, you'll create exactly that experience for yourself. If you believe you only deserve to have a certain amount of money, you'll block more from arriving! Whatever your beliefs may be, they are your truth and you will subconsciously create evidence to support that truth over and over again until you learn to do things differently.

The good news is that you can learn to use the Law of Attraction to improve your financial situation - and, it will be much easier than you might think!

Assignment for the Day: Write down ten beliefs you have about money. Focus on both positive beliefs and negative ones. The goal is to be aware of the beliefs you do have and how they help, or hinder, you from attracting more money.

Day 2 – How Is Lack Formed?

Yesterday, we explored the ways the Law of Attraction works to create your life, including your financial situation. You now know that your thoughts, emotions and beliefs have the power to attract a more abundant lifestyle – or more lack.

What is lack and how does it appear in your life, anyway?

Lack is the condition of not having something. In other words, lack is the absence of something. But the absence of exactly "what" may surprise you. Lack is not the absence of money, or health, or love. Those are just the symptoms of lack.

At its core, lack is simply the blockage of energy.

EVERYTHING IS ENERGY!

When you experience lack of any kind, you are cutting off the natural flow of energy through your life. This can affect much more than your financial situation. In fact, you may notice that when you lack one thing, you usually lack other things too. Your relationships may be more strained or distant. Or, you may experience poor health, lower energy, financial difficulties, or even appliance or vehicle breakdowns. None of this is a coincidence. When you block the flow of abundance, it can manifest in many different forms.

How does this blockage get started? By focusing on what you do not have, or what you do not want. Though it sounds like a bad joke, lack is formed when you focus continuously on lack!

Every time you worry about your financial situation, agonize over a shortage of money, or feel stressed about your bills, you attract the experience of lack into your life. The more you think about things and experiences you don't have, the more you'll attract an absence or blockage of the things you want.

This creates a nasty cycle, in which you can remain stuck for years. If you focus on lack, you create more lack. This, in turn, makes you focus even more on lack, which creates even more lack – and on it goes indefinitely.

It gets even worse, too. Focusing obsessively on the lack in one area of your life can attract lack into other areas of your life, even if they are unrelated. Next thing you know, your entire life is in a major funk and you have no idea how it got so bad.

If you're stuck in one of these funks right now, don't worry! Turning it around is a simple matter of identifying the things you're doing that are creating more lack - and learning how to focus more on abundance.

Assignment for the Day: Make a list of ten things in your life you have an abundance of right now. All around you there is abundance – water, air, beauty, etc. Open yourself to seeing the abundance you already have in your life.

Day 3 – Thoughts and Emotions that Attract Lack

Are you starting to see how pervasive a focus on lack can be? The more you lend your attention and energy to the existence of lack, the more you fuel it!

What exactly do I mean by "lending your attention and energy to the existence of lack?" There are specific thoughts and emotions that create lack and make it grow stronger in your life.

Here they are, in no particular order:

- Fear
- Anxiety
- Helplessness
- Hopelessness
- Pessimism
- Doubt
- Frustration
- Worry
- Jealousy
- Resentment

Every time you choose one of these focuses, you create more lack. In order to turn lack into abundance, you have to avoid investing in these negative emotions. That's not easy to do, I know. This is particularly true when you are feeling stressed by financial issues, as your natural tendency is to obsess over them and to try to find a solution. But every time you allow yourself to feel these emotions, you keep making matters worse.

There are two things you can do to prevent these emotions from creating more lack:

1) **Avoid sinking into feelings like those described above.** As soon as you notice yourself starting to feel stressed or worried about money, immediately shift your focus to something else. You can engage in a bit of self-talk if it helps; say something like, "There's no point worrying about something I can't control, so I'm going to focus on something that makes me feel good." Then spend time on unrelated activities.

You don't need to ignore financial crises or shirk your responsibilities. Rather, give these issues the attention they require and do what you can to make them better. If it makes you feel better to get a second job or refinance/consolidate your loans, do it.

But most important is to avoid investing negative emotions into these issues as you work to resolve them. Stay as detached as you can while doing what you have to do.

2) **Begin directing more positive emotions toward your financial situation.** Even if you have to engage in a bit of fantasizing in order to do so, you need to get some positive emotions flowing so you can attract more abundance!

There are many ways to do this, but one that always works for me is to keep affirming, "I always have more than enough money for everything I need." Just keep saying it over and over again, allowing yourself to feel confident and happy that your financial needs are being met. This is also a good thing to do when you notice you're starting to feel worried or frightened about not having enough money. Just immediately turn the focus around and say, "I ALWAYS have more than enough money for EVERYTHING I need." (Say it with power and conviction in your voice, and really believe that it is so.)

As you begin shifting your focus from negative emotions to positive emotions, you should start to notice your financial situation also shifting to a better place. You might receive an unexpected check in the mail, you might get a bonus or pay raise at work, or you may even notice you're starting to receive unexpected gifts from individuals or companies.

These are great signs that it's working! Keep replacing negative emotions with positive as often as possible and you'll keep the good energy flowing – which will keep inspiring greater and greater change in your life.

Assignment for the Day: Take five minutes to daydream! Sit quietly for five minutes and visualize what your life will be like when you have the money you desire. Get very detailed with your daydream to the point where you can feel yourself being excited, pleased, and at peace. Each time you daydream, add more details to your vision to help it feel even more real.

Day 4 − Activities that Intensify Lack

Are you starting to feel a shift in your financial situation yet? If not, be sure to keep choosing the positive emotions as often as possible. It may take a little time to notice changes taking place, but the end result is well worth it!

Today we're going to cover some destructive habits and activities that contribute to lack, and offer helpful suggestions for turning them around.

To start, I'd like to ask you a question: How do you treat your money?

If money were a person in your life, would he or she feel honored and loved, or, would your money feel abused, neglected and disrespected?

If you're like most people, your relationship with money could probably use a little tender loving care. Therefore, attracting more money into your life means learning to treat money with respect and kindness.

I know, you're thinking, "What? Respect and kindness for an inanimate object? Why?"

The answer is simple: money is not an inanimate object at all. It is energy, remember? Even more importantly, money is a projection of your energy. That means it is a part of you and it has a life and intelligence all its own.

If someone treated you the way you treat your money, you probably wouldn't stick around for more abuse, would you?

Money won't either.

Therefore, it is crucial to avoid these habits and activities where your money is concerned:

- Excessive spending
- Excessive debt
- Reckless disregard for the importance of money
- No savings plan
- Financial disorganization
- Poor planning

You see, the problem isn't that you don't have enough money. The true problem is that you are not managing your money in a way that attracts more of it!

Here are the best things you can do to begin honoring your money (and attracting more!).

1) **Begin a savings plan immediately.** It doesn't matter if you can only spare a dollar or two each week, but begin putting money into a savings account right away. And do not touch that money for any reason! This step is very important because it puts you into the mindset of "having money" – even if the amount you have isn't a lot yet. The more you do this, the wealthier you're going to feel as you remember that you're not "living on the edge."

2) **Avoid spending money on anything that doesn't contribute value to your life.** Do you really need that cute purse when you've already got a closet full of them? Do you really need more "toys"

that will only gather dust when you tire of them in a few weeks? Instead, begin spending your money on things that will help you to grow and deepen as an individual. Buy books to expand your knowledge. Invest in business courses or career development programs. Better yet, begin contributing money to investment programs so it can grow and eventually work for you.

This doesn't mean you can't enjoy the occasional treat. You can still enjoy nice things, but be very choosy about what they are and how often you buy them.

3) **Get organized.** If you haven't balanced your checkbook in ages, or you have no idea how much debt you have, figure it out and create a plan for paying it off. The point of this exercise is not to make you feel bad, but to take responsibility for your financial situation. Trust me - you'll feel much better when you have a clear understanding of where you stand right now, and a solid plan for getting somewhere better.

Remember, you don't have to do everything all at once. Starting small is okay. Eventually it all adds up!

Assignment for the Day: Open a savings account, balance your checkbook and/or review your debt and make a plan of action to get rid of it.

Day 5 – Forming an Abundance Mindset

By now, you should have a solid understanding of the ways you've been creating lack in your life and the activities and habits that only make it worse.

Today we're going to cover how to develop an abundance mindset so you can stay focused on attracting greater prosperity into your life.

An abundance mindset is pretty much the opposite of a lack mindset, and it's easy to switch from one to the other – with a little conscious choice.

There are three main steps that can help you create an abundance mindset:

1) **Give all of your attention and energy to abundance.** Remember, you need to avoid contributing energy and emotion to lack. Now you've got to start giving all the energy and emotion you can to abundance!

Here's how: As often as you can, keep aware of the abundance surrounding you. Look at your home and all the possessions within it, and marvel at how wealthy you really are. Feel grateful for all you have, and affirm that more is on the way.

Also, be sure to notice abundance in the world around you. See how nature blooms and grows so effortlessly, and gaze in awe at store shelves that are loaded with anything you could ever want! Abundance is everywhere if you simply open your eyes to it!

2) Believe it's possible to have more than you can imagine. You're probably used to thinking of your financial situation in very limited ways. While you realize that you earn money from a job or business, you might have difficulty seeing any other way for money to come to you. Acknowledge daily that the universe has unlimited options for sending more money into your life. Decide on a sum of money you'd like to receive in the near future, and then begin affirming that it is on the way to you. Don't worry about how it will arrive. Just believe that it will find a way to enter your life.

3) Expect to receive. Your expectations are very powerful! If you expect to have a limited amount of money, that's exactly what will happen. Instead, start expecting more money to come to you from many different sources. Affirm daily, "Today I expect great things to happen! Money, success and abundance in all forms will find their way to me effortlessly and quickly!" Then be on the lookout for great opportunities – and grab them when they arrive!

Do you see how easy it is to shift your focus from lack to abundance now? It's really just a matter of what you choose to focus on and invest in emotionally. However, there are also specific actions you can take that will help.

Assignment for the Day: Make a list of 10 things for which you are grateful for (a home for your family, a working car, support of your friends, etc).

Day 6 – Activities that Increase Abundance

You're really moving along now, aren't you? You now know what NOT to do if you want to avoid creating more lack, and you've learned some simple mental and emotional techniques that can help attract more abundance into your life.

Here are a few suggestions of physical actions that can begin attracting more abundance into your life.

1) **Do what you love.** The more time you spend feeling good, the more positive emotion you contribute to the creation of your life. This is true in relation to your financial situation, but also all other areas of your life.

Be sure to make a habit of doing the things you really love to do. This can be anything from pursuing creative hobbies to reading inspiring books. Or, it can simply mean spending more quality time with friends and family and making your own self-care a high priority. If it makes you feel happy, fulfilled, healthy and relaxed, do it as often as possible!

2) **Open gateways for prosperity to enter your life.** Are you doing everything you can to help the universe send more money your way? Or are you disallowing abundance by refusing to take action? The universe can find many ways to boost your abundance, but it can do this more easily if you take action to invite greater opportunities. Possible action steps might include: applying for a better-paying job,

buying a lottery ticket, networking with successful people, sharing your talents and skills with the world, and anything else that will create an opening for abundance to enter your life.

Most importantly, do these things without attaching specific expectations to them. Instead, allow the actions themselves to be fun and enjoyable. Do them because you enjoy doing them, without expecting them to pay off in any other way. When you do this, you are "allowing" lots of great things into your life – including money and abundance in many forms.

3) **Don't worry about the "how."** We're so used to trying to figure everything out on our own that it can be hard to detach from "how" abundance will come to you. Don't try to brainstorm money-making activities or focus obsessively on how to bring in more money. Instead, let the universe work on your behalf. Decide how much money you'd like to have in the immediate future, and then ask the universe to lead you to the best opportunities for attracting it. Not only will you discover better opportunities than you could hunt down on your own, you'll probably enjoy them much more too!

These three steps may seem very simple, but they hold great power because they send a strong message to the universe that you are ready, willing and open to receiving greater abundance into your life – without grasping desperately at it.

Assignment for the day: Make a list of three things you enjoy doing that could add joy to your life if you made

the regular habits (walking after dinner, painting, reading before bed).

Spend time doing something you love doing. The more you feel good, the faster you will manifest what you want. Doing things you love, even simple things like listening to music, reading, talking to a friend, etc, can boost your energy and make you an even stronger money magnet.

Day 7 – Shifting Into an Abundant Reality

By now you've got a solid idea of the thoughts, emotions and actions that you should avoid at all costs in order to banish lack from your life forever. You've also got some clear, simple steps you can begin taking right away to begin attracting more abundance into your life.

But did you know that you can instantly create change by simply shifting into an abundant reality?

Right now, you are living *from* a specific reality. Often times, your reality isn't exactly what you want it to be. You don't have as much money as you'd like to have, and perhaps you've got lack in other areas too. In your mind, this is your "truth" – it's the perspective you live from in every moment of every day. Right?

But, what if you could change this perspective simply by changing your mindset? You can!

You can do this by thinking, feeling and acting like you would if your reality actually were different.

How would you think, feel and act if you had all the money you wanted? How would you think, feel and act if you were successful, happy and content with your life?

I bet it would be different than you think, feel and act right now! Am I right?

Starting immediately, I want to encourage you to think, feel and act like a person who is already living the life he or she wants to be living. Make list of words that describe how you would feel in this new reality. Examples:

- Happy
- Secure
- Wealthy
- Content
- Confident
- Fulfilled
- Passionate
- Alive
- Joyful
- Grateful
- Relaxed
- Peaceful

Keep this list of words handy, and then start thinking, feeling and acting that way as often as possible!

Now, keep in mind that you'll probably feel strange doing this at the beginning. It will feel almost like you're acting in a play, or like you are lying to yourself. That's normal, because your current self-image won't match up to the new self-image you're trying to adopt. That's okay!

The more you do this, the more comfortable you're going to get with it, and eventually your physical circumstances are going to start shifting in a new direction. This does work.

Just keep at it as often as you can, consciously choosing to live from your new reality. Become the person who is living the life you want to be living, and you will create that life for yourself.

More than anything else, know that using the Law of Attraction to improve any area of your life is as simple as learning to think, feel and act in different ways.

The way your life is right now is not an accident. It resulted from very specific things you did to create your circumstances. This is not a statement meant to make you feel bad about your past actions and decisions, but rather to show you that you have the power to choose different and better circumstances!

Knowing what you know now, you can call in much more abundant, passionate, fulfilling life circumstances and never feel like a victim again.

Assignment for the Day: Make a list of words that describe your new abundant "reality."

On a Side Note:

How Gratitude Can Help You Attract More Money

Gratitude is one emotion that works hand in hand with the Law of Attraction, especially where money is concerned. Where financial lack is present, there is a blockage of energy – some form of resistance is preventing the natural flow of abundance into the person's life.

This can be difficult to understand by traditional lines of thought. Perhaps you are used to thinking of money as a tangible object that you have to obtain, like most people do. However, with the Law of Attraction, there is nothing to obtain. Rather, you need to *allow* things to be.

"Allowing," as it relates to the Law of Attraction, means being in a state of non-resistance. In other words, not blocking the flow of abundance or goodness into your life. Unfortunately, a focus on lack or on struggle will automatically create blockages.

Gratitude is one easy way to dissolve those blockages and get the flow moving again. Below are three ways to use gratitude to attract more money into your life:

1) **Be grateful for the money you have now.**

This is obvious, but it's something that people often overlook when they've focused on lack for too long. No matter how little money you have right now, you need to move yourself into a state of appreciation and gratitude for having it at all. If it helps, you can remind yourself that some people have far less than you do.

When you pay bills, take a moment to appreciate the product or service that created it. You have already received something in return for that money, so feel grateful about being able to give something back.

2) **Be grateful for the money you can't yet see.**

Even though you may be used to focusing on lack with fearful or anxious thoughts, begin focusing on it with gratitude. Affirm that even though you can't see the flow of abundance in your life yet, you do know it's there. Marvel at the way the universe allows you to create your own reality through the power of perception, and affirm your desire to expand your awareness of the abundance all around you.

3) **Be grateful for all forms of abundance.**

Abundance comes in many forms, not just monetary wealth. Make it a daily habit to express your gratitude and appreciation for the wonderful things and people in your life. Be thankful for your loved ones and friends, your job, your pets, and anything else you can think of. Affirm that it all comes from the same flow of abundance that money comes from, and by allowing more of all forms of abundance, you will also be allowing more money to enter your life.

HOW TO ATTRACT IDEAL RELATIONSHIPS

Day 1 – What is the Law of Attraction and How Does it Affect My Relationships?

Over the next 7 days, we're going to cover some great information that will help you to attract better relationships into your life or to improve the ones you already have. You'll find that the information is geared more toward romantic relationships, but it can easily be applied to any other kind of relationships as well.

First, let's go over exactly what the Law of Attraction is and how it applies to your relationships.

The Law of Attraction works according to your thoughts, emotions and beliefs. Your thoughts trigger your emotions and your emotions emit a "signal" to the universe, which then responds by returning corresponding experiences and events into your life. Basically, whatever you tend to focus on the most is what you'll attract into your life – including the types of people surrounding you.

Take a moment right now and think about the people in your life. Are your family members, friends, co-workers and associates the types of people you want to connect with? Or do you feel like you must have been dropped from a helicopter into a group of people you have nothing in common with?

What about your significant other? Do you have a loving, intimate connection with another person, or are you still waiting for the right person to come along?

Believe it or not, these circumstances are no accident. Your connections with the people around you (or the absence of the person/people you're still waiting for) are usually the result of your mental and emotional states on a day-to-day basis.

If you are having a difficult time believing this concept, it is likely because most of us create our lives by default. We don't purposely try to create problems and the other situations we don't want – we just don't know how to prevent them from developing.

The Law of Attraction simply gives you what you ask for – even if you don't realize you're asking!

Besides your mental and emotional states, your beliefs also come into play, either blocking or accepting the things you've asked for.

This concept is important to understand because, even when you think you're emitting the "right" energy to attract something you want, your beliefs might still be holding it back.

If you don't believe you deserve loving, harmonious relationships, you will subconsciously block them from forming! If you believe that other people can't be trusted, or they're deceptive, or they are all out to hurt and betray you, you will push them away – even if that doesn't apply to the majority of people you meet.

The subconscious mind works in mysterious ways!

Assignment for the Day: Make a list of ten positive beliefs you have about relationships as well as ten negative beliefs. Which of your negative beliefs are creating obstacles that are keeping you from having the relationships you desire?

Day 2 – Reflecting Your Relationship With Yourself

Now that you understand how the Law of Attraction is activated by your thoughts, emotions and beliefs, you may be asking yourself what on earth you must have been thinking to have attracted some of your previous or current relationships.

Remember, it's usually done by default, so don't get too down on yourself about it.

Believe it or not, all of your relationships are simply a reflection of your relationship with yourself. Have you ever noticed a correlation between the way other people treat you and the way you treat yourself?

Think about it for a minute.

If you constantly find yourself surrounded by people who disrespect you or mistreat you, think about how you treat yourself on a regular basis. Are you hard on yourself when you make mistakes? Do you demand a lot from yourself? Do you push yourself harder than you need to, or neglect nurturing and caring for yourself?

If most of the people in your life don't seem to care about you or really love you, ask yourself if that is true of your relationship with yourself too.

Take a few minutes to jot down some insights about your relationships with others. Include your family members, spouse (or ex-spouses or partners), children, friends, co-workers, colleagues, and so on.

Write down the ways they usually relate to you, and then compare those actions and attitudes with the way you usually treat yourself.

I bet you'll be surprised to see a lot of correlations there!

Now, take a few minutes to think about how you'd like to be treated. What would you like your relationships to be like? How would you like others to treat you?

And, the most important question: Are you willing to start treating yourself the same way?

Something truly amazing happens when you do this. Other people start seeing you in a different light, and treating you in accordance with how you treat yourself!

I know it probably seems unbelievable that you can change how others relate to you just by changing the way you treat yourself - but it's true!

All relationships in your life are a direct reflection of your relationship with yourself.

Now, what about the absence of relationships? What if you're still waiting for Mr. or Ms. Right to come walking into your life? What does that mean?

Usually, it means you are not open to a healthy, intimate relationship (or possibly the timing isn't quite right yet).

For starters, ask yourself if you really believe that you deserve an intimate relationship with another person. Are you frightened about trusting again? Are you afraid of getting your heart broken? Do you distrust your ability to tell a "good one" from a "bad one"? Ah, alarm bells are going off in your head right now, aren't they?

If not, you may just need to do a little further exploration before you'll know for sure why you're blocking an intimate relationship – but a reason does exist, I assure you.

Assignment for the Day: Do the exercise outlined above. Write a list of the common occurrences you experience in your relationships. Look through your list and notice if the way others treat you is similar to the way you treat, and speak to, yourself.

Day 3 – Wholeness from Within

Have you discovered some insights about your relationships with others (or about the lack of relationships you thought you wanted)? Most likely, you're beginning to see how your own thoughts, feelings and beliefs have attracted certain kinds of people into your life – and repelled other kinds away from you.

More importantly, you understand how powerful your relationship with yourself is when it comes to its impact on the treatment you receive from others.

Today, we're going to explore the concept of wholeness, especially as it applies to romantic relationships.

If I had a nickel for every person who expected a romantic relationship to be the answer to making them whole, I'd be a millionaire! Logically, you probably realize that no one else can make you truly "whole." You are already whole.

Yet, if you still haven't found your "soul mate," you probably feel empty somehow, like something is missing. That sense of emptiness is what usually makes people relentlessly search for the love of their life, hoping to find the missing connection that will finally make them feel "whole."

You've heard the expression "two halves of a whole," right? Many people think the same concept applies here, but that is a complete crock. Pardon my bluntness. I blame Hollywood and fairytales for making us believe that we have to be locked in a passionate embrace in order to feel like our lives are complete.

Don't get me wrong, romance is awesome! Love and passion are right up there on the list of the greatest things on earth. But you do not need a passionate love affair in order to feel like your life is joyful and meaningful!

Do you know what really causes that feeling of incompleteness? Your perception that you must be involved in a relationship in order to feel complete. According to the Law of Attraction, such a belief must be true! If you persist in believing that you won't be whole until you find Mr. or Ms. Right, you will make that your reality.

The problem with making this belief your reality is that you place an awful lot of pressure on any potential partner that enters your life. Even if you don't say it, they can sense that you are depending on them to make you feel whole and happy. That's not really their job,. It's yours!

In order to attract the love of your life, you need to be whole and happy already – before they enter the picture.

There's a good reason for this. Whenever you try to bring something into your life through the principles of the Law of Attraction, your emotional frequency emits a signal to the universe. When you feel like you desperately "need" something in order to be happy and whole, you emit the reality of "neediness" and you attract others that feel needy as well.

On the other hand, when you emit a frequency of happiness and fulfillment about your life, you attract other whole, happy people – including one that seeks a life partner.

So, be sure to do whatever you can to fill yourself up from within! Do things you love. Create a life you love, even if Mr. or Ms. Right hasn't shown up yet. When he/she does, you'll want to be ready to welcome him/her with open arms!

Assignment for the Day: Do you feel a void in your life which you hope a romantic partner will fill? If so, make a list of five things you believe a romantic partner would bring into your life. Now, look over your list and ask yourself, how can I bring those same things into my life now?

Day 4 – Being the Perfect Partner for Your Perfect Partner

Yesterday, we discussed the importance of being whole and happy before your perfect partner shows up, rather than relying on another person to make you feel complete. That's a powerful start, but there are also other things you can do to boost the likelihood of attracting the type of partner you want.

Today, I encourage you to make a detailed list of the qualities and traits you'd like your perfect partner to have. What do you imagine he or she will look like? What type of personality will he or she have? What aspirations or ambitions for the future will he or she have?

Use as much detail as you can, covering everything from career to personality, spiritual beliefs, physical appearance and beyond.

When you're finished, read over the list. Did you include everything you want your perfect partner to have?

Now comes the fun part. Go back over that list and check off any of the traits and descriptions that fit YOU.

Do you have the same type of spiritual beliefs you want your partner to have? Do you have the same type of personality? Do you have the same level of goals and ambitions in life?

Don't worry if you don't have all the traits – that's not the point of this exercise. Instead, notice how many you do have, compared to how many you don't. Then ask yourself this question:

Would I be the perfect partner for this person I want to attract?

Obviously, you and your partner are two separate people, so there will be differences in your personalities and goals. But, if the differences are too great, what makes you think your perfect partner would be attracted to someone he or she has almost nothing in common with?

If the traits and qualities on your list are important to you, you need to start developing them within yourself first!

Then, when your perfect partner arrives on the scene, he or she will quickly recognize a kindred soul – and sparks are much more likely to fly. There are other factors involved, of course. But being the perfect partner for your perfect partner is a very big part of it.

Assignment for the Day: Do the exercise mentioned above. Make a very detailed list describing your ideal partner.

Day 5 – How to Attract the Love of Your Life

Are you feeling clearer about the type of person you need to be in order to attract more meaningful relationships?

Today, we're going to talk more about the things you can do to actually begin attracting them. And the very first step is to stop trying to attract your perfect partner!

"What?" you may be asking.

Bear with me; it actually makes sense when you think about it.

The more you obsess about finding your perfect partner, the stronger message of "need" you send to the universe. You'll enter every social situation with the expectation of meeting "The One." If it doesn't happen, you'll feel disappointed and you will send more negative energy to the universe.

Rather than obsessing about finding someone, you have to be willing to let go of your expectations. You must detach yourself from thinking about how and when it will all come about.

That's not easy to do, I know. But it's necessary; otherwise you continue to convey neediness and desperation to the universe.

Rather than walking into every situation with the expectation of meeting "The One," make it your mission to simply enjoy meeting interesting people. Think of them as friends only, not potential love matches. If sparks happen to fly with someone you meet, great! See where it might lead. But don't expect to have a match.

It's also important to create openings for potential partnerships to form. After all, you want to make it more likely that your perfect partner will find you, right. That means engaging in activities that your potential partner would also be likely to engage in.

You don't have to go nuts with this and join dozens of clubs or exhaust yourself with excessive social activities. Your perfect partner can find you anywhere, really. But do what you can to increase the likelihood, within reason.

I'm frequently asked if it's possible to attract someone specific with the Law of Attraction. My answer is always the same: Yes, but only if that person feels attracted to you too! If he or she does not want to be with you, you will be wasting your time by trying to force something that isn't going to happen. Please don't do that to yourself.

If you have feelings for someone that doesn't feel the same about you or if you've broken up with someone who does not want to get back together – find a way to let them go. You cannot use the Law of Attraction to force them to want you. You just can't.

Instead, be willing to believe that there is someone better for you out there - someone who has many of the same traits as this other person, but who will be an even better match for you.

Assignment for the Day: Come up with three new ways you can open yourself up to connect with new people. Choose situations that will be comfortable to you and will, not just allow you to meet new people, but also bring you pleasure. As an example, rather than simply going to a single's event for the sake of meeting a potential romantic partner, why not connect with people who are interested in a passion or hobby you have wanted to make a bigger part of your life?

Day 6 – Making Room for Your Perfect Partner

You should now have a solid understanding of the way your thoughts, beliefs and emotions attract certain kinds of people into your life and how other relationships mirror your relationship with yourself. You also know the importance of being whole and happy on your own, as well as the importance of being the person your perfect partner would want to be with. Finally, you've now got some clear ideas of things you can do to help bring him or her into your life.

But, what will you do when he or she gets here? Is there room for this new person in your life?

Let's face it - new relationships take some adjustment before you settle into a comfortable routine. If your life circumstances are rigid and restricted, you may have a difficult time shifting them to make room for a new relationship.

You can begin the process now, however, so your perfect partner will slip into your life with barely a glitch. There are three main areas you should give some attention to:

1) **Time.** Do you have time for a committed relationship? Do you work a lot or have other demands on your time?

One thing that many of us do when we get involved in a new relationship is drop everything else. It's understandable because, when we're in love, we feel so happy that we don't want that feeling to end. So we might neglect our friends and family members, or even our work or other obligations for a while, which isn't healthy.

Try to avoid this by instead making room in your schedule for your perfect partner. When he or she arrives, how much time will you spend together? How much time do your other obligations require?

You don't have to get too detailed with this, but do your best to make room in your schedule for the new relationship you're attracting. When you do, you create a space for it to arrive in your life!

2) **Physical surroundings.** The same thing goes for your physical surroundings. Is the passenger seat of your car loaded with so much stuff that no one else can sit there? Is your home crammed to the ceilings with your own belongings with little room for someone else's belongings?

Go through the same process of making room for your perfect partner in your physical surroundings as you did with your schedule, and you'll create a space for him or her to become part of your life.

3) **Emotional.** Finally, are you emotionally ready to welcome your perfect partner into your life? You may think you are, but I want you to have a clear picture of what it will be like to share your life with another person.

Are you ready to connect intimately and to communicate deeply with another person? Are you ready to open your heart and to trust someone else?

If not, you will find a way to sabotage any new relationship that enters your life. To avoid this, be sure to strengthen yourself emotionally beforehand. One good way to do this is to visualize yourself feeling confident and strong from within while you open your heart and share your life with another person.

These three areas are key, but the point is to create a space in all areas of your life. That way, when your perfect partner does come along, he or she will fit right in.

Assignment for the Day: Now that you have made a list of the things you are looking for in a partner, write out a description of how your ideal relationship will unfold. How much time would you like to spend with your partner? Where will the two of you live? Will you move in together? How does sharing your life look like in your mind's eye? The point of this exercise is for you to define exactly what you are looking for, so you are more easily able to manifest it.

Day 7 – Living From Your Perfect Partnership

Today we're going to explore the concept of living from the reality you want to attract. In this case, living from the reality of already having your perfect partner in your life.

One powerful way to work with the Law of Attraction is to consciously be the person who has what you want. We've already discussed doing this on a physical level by being the person your perfect partner would want to be with and engaging in the activities that your perfect partner would also be likely to engage in.

This time, however, I'm referring more to your mental and emotional state as you go about your daily activities. Are you thinking, feeling and acting like a person who already has the perfect partnership?

Or are you constantly focusing on how lonely and isolated you feel? Do you gaze jealously at other couples, wondering impatiently where your partner is? Do you feel sorry for yourself when you hear love songs on the radio or watch a romantic movie?

All of these things are sure to keep you living from the perspective of not having the relationship you desire! If you turn this around, you are much more likely to attract what you want.

Here's what I suggest:

- Beginning immediately, give your best effort to thinking, feeling and acting like a person who is involved in a loving, committed relationship.

- Feel loved, cherished, happy, and secure.

- Be happy for other couples when you see them because you know the joy of feeling connected and intimate with a significant other.

- When you watch romantic movies or hear love songs on the radio, let your heart lift with joy and gratitude for the way they inspire you.

- Affirm as often as possible that your perfect partner is already here and will enter your life at the perfect time. Feel grateful and happy about it because you know it's true!

That's as far as your thoughts and emotions are concerned, but living from your perfect partnership also involves taking the actions that you would take if you were already involved with Mr. or Ms. Right.

Would you eat in nice restaurants? Would you take long, leisurely walks on the beach? Would you go out dancing?

Whatever activities you picture yourself doing with a lover, begin doing them yourself. If it makes you too uncomfortable to do them alone, ask a friend or family member to join you.

The more time you spend living from the perspective of your new reality, the more quickly and easily your current reality will shift to include the things you really want.

Attracting your perfect partner is no different than attracting anything else you want in life. Simply get clear about what you want, make room for it, and focus your thoughts, feelings, beliefs and activities in such a way that pulls it right into your life.

Assignment for the Day: Make a list of 15 things—five ways you would feel, five ways you would act, and five things you would do—if you were in your ideal relationship. Now, look at your list and ask yourself, how can I experience those things right now?

On a Side Note

How to Allow With the Law of Attraction

When you think of "allowing" in relation to the Law of Attraction, you probably think of being in a state where you are ready to receive the things you have asked for. This is true, but it actually goes a lot deeper than that.

Allowing actually means to be in a state of non-resistance. You may be surprised to learn what the states of resistance are – because you may be entering into them without realizing it.

Fear, worry, anxiety, frustration and impatience

These states automatically place you into a place of resistance because you are doubting that the Law of Attraction will work for you, focusing more on what you don't want, and affirming that you don't yet have the things that will make you feel happy and content. You begin emitting a strong frequency of lack and disbelief, which the Law of Attraction must return to you in some form!

When you are in these types of mental and emotional states, you are blocking anything good from coming into your life. In order to turn it around, you need to move yourself into a more relaxed, positive frame of mind and emotion.

Rather than worrying and obsessing about what is wrong in your life, begin focusing more on the good things surrounding you, and all the wonderful things that will be coming to you soon. You don't have to know when they'll arrive, just affirm that they will and that you will be ready and waiting when they do.

It may be challenging to switch your focus when you get caught up in emotions like these, but it's crucial if you want to move back into a state of allowing.

Then, focus more of your attention on purposely staying in a state of allowing. You can do this by deliberately choosing more positive thoughts and emotions, meditating, visualizing and using affirmations.

The techniques don't really matter. All that really matters is that you choose to move yourself from a negative focus to a positive one.

If you struggle to move your focus, find some activities that will help you. Watch a funny movie on television or buy a DVD of your favorite sitcom episodes. Read uplifting books and spend time with successful and dynamic people. Think about the day you got married, the first time you fell in love, the births of your children, or any moving experience from your past. Buy a book of jokes and get into the habit of reading them daily – and be sure to have a strong belly laugh.

By taking conscious control of your moods and mindset, you will be able to stay in a state of allowing much more frequently, which should help you improve your results with the Law of Attraction.

How to Attract Your Best Health

Day 1 – What is the Law of Attraction and How Does It Affect My Health?

Have you ever wondered why some people enjoy ongoing good health while others deal with a seemingly never-ending string of illness throughout their lifetime? Is it determined by genetics? Lifestyle? Or, is it as Law of Attraction experts tell us – we create the state of our body according to our thoughts and beliefs.

The Law of Attraction responds to your thoughts, feelings, and beliefs. In a nutshell, whatever you focus on the most is what you tend to attract into your life. Focus on positive things, and you'll usually attract positive experiences; focus more on the negative side and you'll attract more negative outcomes.

The reason for this phenomenon is quite simple: your emotional state emits a specific "frequency" of vibration to the universe and the universe responds by sending corresponding situations and events into your life.

But is that always true when it comes to our health and well-being? Does that mean that people who get cancer were focused on getting cancer? Not necessarily. More often, the process is a subconscious one – and not specifically targeted. In other words, illness often develops as a result of many factors, such as lifestyle habits, the overall mindset a person holds most often, and yes, genetics play a part also.

If your state of health isn't what you want it to be, I won't presume to tell you that you brought it upon yourself by "thinking wrong." Obviously, there is much more to it for most of us. The truth is, you may never know exactly why this illness has come into your life, but you do have a choice when it comes to how you react to it. Will you see it as a punishment? Your cross to bear? A learning experience? A challenge to be overcome? The perspective from which you view any illness or disease will usually inspire different thoughts, feelings and actions, which will bring about a different outcome.

The most important thing to understand is that when it comes to health and well-being, there are no cookie-cutter answers that will help everyone. What works for one person may not work for another.

Listen closely to your own inner guidance. You will know intuitively when something is right for you or when it is not. If something doesn't seem to fit, it's probably not right for you at this time. At the very least, I hope to offer you some food for thought and helpful information that will change the way you perceive your body and the ways your thoughts, emotions and beliefs affect it.

Assignment for the Day: Give some thought as to how you are feeling about your current health. Often times, we don't pay much attention to our health, until there is a problem. Are there things you want to change? If so, do you believe they can be healed, or improved, by changing the way you feel?

Day 2 – How Illness and Disease ("Dis-Ease") Form in Your Body

To say that illness is always the result of negative thinking would be a bit presumptuous, because the Law of Attraction responds to more than your thoughts. Even so, why then do positive people end up getting sick too? According to the Law of Attraction, positive people should always be healthy, right?

Unfortunately, that is not usually the case. Rather, let's gear our focus along the lines of Eastern tradition, which views illness and disease ("Dis-Ease") as blockages in the currents of energy running through the human body.

We know that everything in the universe is composed of energy at its most basic level. That includes everything around us as well as our own bodies. Since our thoughts, emotions and beliefs emit energetic vibrations to the universe, it stands to reason that these energy currents can also affect the state of our bodies.

Let's use the example of a positive person who becomes ill. Though it seems like they should enjoy great health because they are always emitting positive thoughts, we also need to look at their emotional state, their beliefs, and their habits.

Just because a person is positive doesn't mean he or she doesn't worry obsessively, hold fears or beliefs about poor health, or engage in habits that could compromise his or her health. When you consider these many different facets, you easily see how factors other than your thoughts matter.

From a purely energetic standpoint, illness can usually be detected as a blockage in the natural flow of energy through the body. Blockages can be caused by many different things, but common causes include negative thoughts and emotions, as well as limiting beliefs and stress.

Most often, this occurs when the natural flow of energy through the body is clouded by thoughts of lack, fear, worry, stress or even negative habits. As a result, a disturbance begins to form in the current of energy. Think of it like a pipe that begins to build residue inside. If enough residues build up, the flow of water through the pipe can become blocked and will eventually cut off altogether. Once this occurs, the blockage must be cleared before the flow can be restored.

The same thing happens with our bodies. First, the blockage is minor so we don't pay much attention to it. Over time, if the causes are not addressed, illness will form.

Illness and disease are simply signs from your body that something isn't right. A blockage has formed and needs to be dissolved.

Regardless of whether you believe you caused an illness to form or that there were other contributing factors, only you can say whether you can heal it and go on to live a healthy, vibrant life. Understand that even people who have been given the direst of prognoses by medical health professionals have somehow found it within themselves to heal completely. Do you believe you have the potential to do the same? As we move through this book, you'll come to realize just how powerful your beliefs can be!

Assignment for the Day: Make a list of all the things you consider to be stressful in your life. After you create the list, go through and ask yourself how your stress is impacting your body. Next, look at which stresses you can eliminate and also new things you can do to help your body relax.

Day 3 – Your Natural State of Abundant Health and Vitality

Perhaps you can remember a time in the past when you enjoyed great health and vitality. You had tons of energy and felt strong and happy. Your body seemed to hum with well-being and you felt invincible.

Sadly, most of us don't experience that feeling except in short bursts throughout our lifetime. Otherwise, we struggle with fatigue, various illnesses, excessive stress and the perception that our bodies are our enemies, always causing problems and not allowing us to do the things we want to do.

But imagine if it could be the other way around. Imagine feeling great the majority of the time, and only experiencing illness on rare occasion. How would we get to this state of being?

Again, since there are many different causes for illness, there is not a magic solution for everyone. However, there are certain mindsets and activities that tend to foster good health more than others. Let's explore a few of them:

1) **Positive emotion.** Quantum physics is beginning to reveal the true power our emotions have over our reality, including the state of our bodies. Positive emotions tend to put us in a state of relaxation, peace, and happiness, while negative emotions create feelings of frustration, anger, and dis-ease – which can trigger illness to form.

To foster a state of well-being, positive emotion is one key that cannot be disregarded. What exactly is positive emotion? States of happiness, gratitude, joy, humor and love seem to be the most powerful.

2) **Attitude and beliefs.** In addition to positive emotion, attitude and beliefs seem to play a big role in the overall health and well-being of a person. If you believe you will get well, you are more likely to recover than someone who accepts a negative prognosis as absolute truth.

Also important is the attitude you hold about your illness. Do you believe it's a punishment of some kind? Do you believe you have terrible luck? Do you believe it's impossible to overcome certain illnesses? Those types of thoughts are more apt to create disharmony in the body.

In addition, the determination to become well again is vital - rather than allowing thoughts of doom and gloom to overtake your focus.

3) **Proper nutrition and rest.** Though our bodies are composed of energy, they are also nourished by nutritious food and clean water (though those are composed of energy too!).

By making sure you eat nutrient rich foods and stay fully hydrated, you give your body the fuel it needs to dissolve blockages and heal.

Getting enough rest is also important because, when

you rest, you free up more energy that your body can devote to healing disharmony and imbalance.

None of these things will guarantee that you'll never get sick, but they certainly contribute to the likelihood of better health!

More than anything else, believe that you deserve abundant good health. Too often we take our illnesses personally, believing we must have done something bad in order to deserve such suffering. Instead, use illness and imbalance as an opportunity to create a healthful lifestyle and bring your thoughts, emotions, beliefs and habits into balance again.

Assignment for the Day: Begin to keep a food and sleep journal. If you spend just 21 days writing down the food you consume and also document how much rest you get, your journal will help you clearly see what you are doing right and what needs to change.

Day 4 – The Wonder of Regeneration

Have you ever marveled at your body's ability to heal itself? You get a cut, it heals. You bruise yourself, it gradually fades away. Even illnesses that were once presumed to be fatal have shown that they are not impossible to heal, either spontaneously or through various treatment options.

Because we are used to thinking of matter as solid and unchangeable, we tend to think of our bodies in the same way. We think of them as lumps of material over which we have no control, except to simply move them around. The reality is that they are not really solid at all when they are viewed on a small scale and with the right equipment.

Your body is like an intelligent machine that is constantly shedding parts of itself and re-growing new parts to take their place. Cells die and new cells are formed all the time. Experts say that we end up with completely new bodies every few years!

Think about what that means. If it's really true that we end up with all new cells and tissues every few years, who's to say that we couldn't replace diseased cells with healthy cells?

Of course, no one really knows the limits of regeneration yet (if there even are any). We do know that certain species of animals can regrow limbs and tails. Could humans do the same? Most Law of Attraction experts seem to think so. In fact, many of them say that the only reason humans haven't done it yet is because we just don't believe it's possible.

In any case, one thing we do know is that we have complete control over our thoughts, feelings, beliefs and actions – and those will trigger the Law of Attraction.

Even if you're not sure if you can regenerate parts of your body, you know you can regenerate your attitude and beliefs, right? Use that as a starting point and expand your beliefs from there.

Take a few minutes right now to clarify your beliefs about regeneration and healing. Do you believe it's possible to heal illnesses, even if they've been with you for a very long time? Do you believe it would be possible for humans to regrow limbs, improve vision, regrow teeth, or heal scars? Why or why not?

It's important to get a clear idea of your beliefs about health and healing, because truly, what you believe is what you will allow into your reality. If you don't believe it, it won't happen. We'll be covering the power of beliefs in more detail shortly, but for now just get a general idea of what you currently believe is possible or impossible.

Assignment for the Day: As suggested, think about, and clarify, your beliefs regarding healing. Do you believe it is possible for you to heal your body? Why or why not?

Day 5 – Calling in a Wave of Healing Energy

Illness is often the result of a blockage of energy in the body. Conversely, good health means that the energy is flowing unimpeded through your body as it should be.

There are many great techniques that can help facilitate this, and below are a few of the most well-known:

1) **Breath work.** In many cultures, breath is believed to be the force of life. Often referred to as *prana, qi,* or *chi,* breath is thought to be the living essence of divinity within us. Breathing techniques are used by spiritual leaders in many traditions to prepare for ceremonies, achieve a deeper state of spirituality, and yes - facilitate healing!

One of the simplest techniques is deep, slow breathing. This means taking full breaths rather than the shallow breathing many of us tend to do on a regular basis. You can do this by inhaling slowly and then allowing the abdomen to expand and then doing the same with your chest. Once your lungs are full, slowly exhale while making a "shhhhh" sound until your lungs are deflated. Then inhale slowly and deeply again, repeating the process as many times as you like. Note: Be sure to do it slowly and pause in between breaths so you don't get lightheaded or dizzy.

2) **Meditation.** It is said that quieting your thoughts and connecting more deeply to your spiritual center can instantly create feelings of peace and well-being,

which will promote healing in the physical body.

If you've never meditated before, don't feel intimidated by it; it's very easy to do! Believe it or not, meditation is as simple as quieting your mind. You can also play soothing music if you like, or burn scented candles and incense, or anything you feel will help you relax.

Whatever you do, don't expect to be able to "shut off your thoughts" right away. Expect to have your mind wander, and simply return it gently to a relaxed focus as often as you need to. Eventually your ability to focus will strengthen and you won't have to take this extra step as often.

3) **Visualization.** Visualization has been used in healing modalities with quite a bit of success in recent years. Patients have visualized healing light dissolving illnesses or even a school of "fish" eating away tumors in their bodies – with surprising results!

The great thing about visualization is that it doesn't matter what images you see in your mind (or even that you see any images at all), but rather how your thoughts make you *feel*. Remember that the Law of Attraction is activated by your emotional state. If you imagine a wave of healing light flowing through your body and dissolving all illness and disharmony, you will emit exactly that type of frequency to the universe.

What should you visualize? Try something like these examples: see illness as a pool of brackish liquid in your body and healing energy as waves of clear water that flow in and wash it away. Or, see illness as a negative belief in need of acknowledgement and healing energy as the force that can resolve pain and transform illness into wholeness and joy. Or, don't focus on illness at all, but rather imagine waves of brilliant white or golden light sweeping over and through every part of your body, washing away all disharmony and disease.

Again, what you see does not matter – only how it makes you feel. So picture something that makes you feel empowered and whole, and really allow yourself to get into those feelings as you perform your visualization.

There are many more ways to call in healing energy, but these are probably the most common. Follow your instincts on which techniques would be right for you, and do what makes you most comfortable. Remember, if you believe it works, it works!

Assignment for the Day: Practice calling in healing energy. If you haven't done it before, try one of the suggestions above. Or, do some research to find a method that feels right for you.

Day 6 – Beliefs and Health

What is a belief, anyway? A belief is a thought that has been repeated and reinforced in your mind so many times that it has become your "truth." It's hard to describe just how deeply beliefs control every aspect of your life!

There's no way to say it any better than this: Whatever you believe is true. Whatever you don't believe is not true. (for you).

That's important as far as the Law of Attraction goes, because you will NOT allow something into your life if you hold a limiting belief about it.

For example, let's say you take all the right actions, think the right thoughts, feel the right emotions and basically do everything in your power to get well. If you don't believe you can heal, you simply won't allow it to happen because your subconscious mind will block it.

The same is true if you don't believe you deserve to be healed. If you hold a perception of an angry or judgmental universe (or God), you may not allow healing to take place because you struggle with feelings of unworthiness or fear.

How do you know if you are holding limiting beliefs? Most often, you'll experience a sense of conflict when you try to embrace a new way of thinking. For example, try repeating this statement: "I believe that I deserve to live an abundant, healthy life."

What happens in your body when you say that? Do you feel

tense, anxious or doubtful?

Try this one: "I believe that I can heal any illness or disharmony that forms in my body."

Any feelings of resistance there?

If so, you've got some work ahead of you in order to turn those limiting beliefs around. Think of limiting beliefs as big boulders sitting squarely in the path that leads to your chosen destination. They cannot be moved or navigated around; they must be removed in order to proceed.

One way to do this is to replace limiting beliefs with positive beliefs. First, of course, you need to have a clear idea of what your limiting beliefs are. Try writing down some statements like those above and following your intuition about which beliefs may be holding you back. Focus on two main things: what you believe you deserve and what you believe is possible.

Once you have some statements to clarify the beliefs, say them out loud and pay close attention to any feelings that come up in your body or any opposing thoughts that pop into your mind. If you experience any reaction like that, it's a sure sign that you've encountered a limiting belief.

When you've got a clear idea of your limiting beliefs, explore them further. Why do you believe them? Were there experiences in your life that caused them and reinforced them? Are you willing to be open to other possibilities?

Believe it or not, turning limiting beliefs around isn't that difficult, it just requires an open and persistent mind. You can do this by creating a new belief that will contradict the limiting one. However, the trick is to make it believable in the way you phrase it.

For example, let's say you have a limiting belief that you cannot heal a disease or condition you were born with. That's a pretty solid belief, especially if it has been reinforced through your entire lifetime by yourself and by others. A good way to get around that and to create a new, empowering belief is to word it something like this: "I believe that miracles happen every day, and I am just as deserving of good health as anyone." Or "I believe that this condition is an opportunity for me to see what I'm truly capable of creating in my life." Or, "I believe that my mind and spirit can choose health and wellness."

What you say doesn't matter. Simply allow words that feel right to you to loosen the rigidity of your limiting beliefs.

Once you've got a statement that feels good to you, say it with confidence and say it often. Eventually, you'll find your mind opening even further to include beliefs that would have once seemed foreign to you.

Finally, keep in mind that you are the one who forms your beliefs – always. Your beliefs may have begun as messages from others in your life, but you can decide to change them at any time. And once you do, you open up a whole new world of possibilities!

Assignment for the Day: Looking at your beliefs is important. Just as important is turning negative beliefs

around, into positive beliefs that feel good to you. Re-read the instructions above and turn a limiting belief you have about your health into one that is empowering, positive, and helpful.

Day 7 – Living From a New Perspective

Hopefully you now understand just how powerful your own thoughts, feelings, beliefs and actions can be when it comes to your health and well-being. Do you also realize that numerous people have been able to heal even the most aggressive conditions, simply because they refused to believe it was impossible to do so? Medical journals are full of unexplainable accounts of healing. Could you be next?

The Law of Attraction responds to your emotional and mental state. You know the importance of thinking and feeling positively, but here is where many people go wrong: they keep shifting back into their old state of *dis-ease*!

They may do well for a few hours, or even a few days, but before long they are focusing on their illness again, talking about their aches and pains, and living from the perspective of a person who is burdened with an illness.

Now, I'm not going to say it's easy to do otherwise. It's tempting to focus on that which displeases us. It's hard not to think about pain when you're experiencing pain. It's hard to feel joyful and happy when you just don't feel well.

But, at the same time, living from a new perspective means finding a way to set the illness aside and to live each moment as a person who is completely well and happy. Even if it means you have to take a trip to "fantasy land" for a while.

Here are some suggestions for doing this:

1) **Gratitude.** Gratitude is a powerful state of mind because it automatically gets you focusing on what's good, rather than on what's bad. You can focus on feeling grateful for the good things you already have, or you can feel grateful for what is coming – as if it were already here.

Be grateful for being completely healed, even if you aren't yet! Shift your mindset and imagine that you have experienced a complete healing. How would you feel about it? Joyful? Awed? Relieved? Down-on-your-knees grateful? Allow yourself to feel that way right now, and you'll help pull such a reality into your current circumstances.

2) **Separate yourself from your pain and discomfort.** This isn't always easy to do, but did you know that there are people who can control pain with the power of their thoughts? In fact, there are cultures that consider this ability a badge of honor. Warriors are tested on their ability to transcend pain by focusing their thoughts. You can learn to do this too!

One simple technique I learned years ago involves detaching from the sensation of pain or discomfort, rather than resisting it. When you resist pain or focus in on it, what happens? It intensifies, right? If you instead mentally and emotionally distance yourself from it and remember that it's simply a sensation in your body, not good or bad, it doesn't seem as difficult to bear. There is an element of acceptance involved here – instead of fighting against pain or allowing it to take over your body and mind, you simply accept that it's there and you can shift your focus to other things.

Again, this isn't always easy to do, especially if you're not used to it. But, with practice, you can get quite proficient at it.

These two techniques are a great start, but most importantly, just make an effort to think, feel, and act as if you had no blockages in your body as often as you can every day. The more you do this, the more you will contribute your energy to exactly that reality.

Assignment for the Day: One of the fastest ways to ease pain is to focus on gratitude. Today, (and every day), write down a list of five things you are grateful for. As you write, feel the emotion behind your words.

On a Side Note:

How to Overcome Negativity from Others

Have you been working hard at improving your own thoughts and emotions, only to encounter rude and negative people in your daily life? The Law of Attraction responds to your thoughts and emotions, but too often it's easy to be influenced by the people that surround you. You may start out in a great mood, but quickly find yourself spiraling down because of negativity being tossed your way by others. What should you do about it?

First, remember that you don't have to absorb other people's moods and attitudes. It is possible to mentally and emotionally step back from them and to put up your guard.

Before you can do that, however, you need to take a more active role in choosing your own mood and mindset. This involves consciously choosing a positive mindset to start the day and repeatedly reinforcing it throughout the day by reciting affirmations, visualizing, choosing positive emotions, and using positive self-talk.

If you're already doing that, you should definitely feel a bit stronger when you encounter negativity. Nonetheless, it can still be unsettling. Here are a few suggestions to help you resist others' negativity.

Override the negativity of others in your own mind. Imagine that you're at work, you're in a good mood, and your coworker comes in, fuming about something that made her angry. She's complaining loudly and threatening to ruin your positive outlook. You can mentally choose to override her negativity with some powerful self-talk, like this, "Wow, she's obviously not having a good day! I feel bad for her, but I don't have to get sucked into the negativity. I choose to stay happy and positive today." It's amazing what you can block out when you really set your mind to it.

"Cancel" out the energy of these negative people. The word "cancel" can be very powerful. Using the same example as above, you could mentally say "CANCEL" every time your coworker says something negative and imagine that your intention blocks any negative energy from entering your mind and mood.

Express love and compassion for negative people. One good way to blot out negativity is to shift immediately into a state of compassion and love. As your coworker rails about her problems, you can mentally send her lots of love and healing thoughts, wishing her the best. Because you're focused more on positive emotions, you won't be absorbing the negative ones!

Remove yourself from the presence of negative people. Finally, if all else fails and you're really struggling to stay positive in the face of negativity, you've got little choice but to sneak away for a while. This may not always be possible, but if you can't do it physically, try your hardest to detach mentally and emotionally.

When it comes right down to it, you are the only one in charge of what you think and feel, regardless of what others may say or do. With a little bit of practice and a lot of determination, you should be able to overcome any negativity others can throw your way.

HOW TO ATTRACT YOUR DREAM JOB

Day 1 – What is the Law of Attraction and How Does it Relate to My Job?

The Law of Attraction is activated by your thoughts, beliefs and emotions, and returns corresponding experiences into your life. If you tend to think and feel positively much of the time, you probably have mostly positive experiences. Likewise, if you tend to think and feel negatively much of the time, you probably have a fair number of negative experiences.

Your beliefs provide the framework for your thoughts and feelings as well as for the things you allow into your life. Even if you think and feel positively much of the time, holding limiting beliefs can block the things you would otherwise attract.

How is your career affected by all of this? There are many ways, but one is the type of work you do for a living.

Most often, we choose our line of work based on a set of beliefs and preferences. Sometimes it may seem that you didn't even choose your work as much as it chose you. Did you make a conscious decision to pursue your current career, or did you kind of fall into it without much conscious decision-making on your part?

It's very common for people to choose a career because of limiting beliefs.

For example, you may have had dreams of one career as a child, but were repeatedly told by parents and other authority figures that it wasn't practical, so you settled for a career with more stability or security. Or you may have felt that your desired career wouldn't be possible because you didn't have the talent or confidence to pursue it, so you chose something you felt you could handle.

No matter what your specific circumstances may be, know that your subconscious thoughts and beliefs play a large role in where you find yourself in your career today.

That may make it sound like it's out of your control, but just the opposite is true! Even if you chose your current career without consciously intending to, you can learn how to shift your thoughts and emotions and alter your beliefs so that you purposely attract a career that suits you better.

Assignment for the Day: Ask yourself how the world would benefit if you had your dream job? Write down your answer. Feel the emotion behind the words you write.

Day 2 – What Your Work Reveals About You

Your job is nothing more than an expression of whom you are while you perform it – either whom you think you are or whom you think you need to be at the time. In other words, your job reveals a lot about *you*. Not only whom you are, but also whom you think you are.

Take a minute now to get a clear mental image of your current job (or previous job if you are unemployed now). What do you like about it? What do you dislike about it? Does it utilize your strengths, or offer a convenient excuse to avoid stepping out of your comfort zones?

If your current or previous jobs don't seem to match whom you think you are, question why that is. It's not random, I assure you!

Jot down as many ideas and insights as you can about how you ended up in your current or previous careers and what they reveal about your mindset at the time.

Pay particular attention to your beliefs about yourself and your capabilities. Does your current or previous work reveal limiting beliefs about your value as a person or your potential for success?

For example, did you choose the job(s) because you didn't believe you could do better? Or because you didn't have a clear idea of what you really wanted? Did you simply go along with what someone else wanted for you? Did you choose your job because of how much it pays?

If you're not really sure, here's a good way to tell. Sometimes your subconscious mind will spill the beans if you read an open-ended statement and let the rest of it come out spontaneously. See if you can use this technique to gain clarity about your work. Take a look at the statement below and write down any answers that come to mind right away. Don't analyze it or try to come up with a good answer, just take the first thing that comes to mind:

- I am in my current career because _____.

Did your answer(s) surprise you? If you didn't receive any insights, write the statement down and set it aside. Focus on something else for a while and then try again. The trick is to catch your subconscious mind off guard and trigger it to provide an answer.

You may think that this stuff doesn't matter, but it's important to understand where your focus was when you entered into a situation that doesn't match what you really want. By doing so, you will be better able to get clear about what you really want and you will be able to develop the right mindset to attract it.

Assignment for the Day: Follow the instructions above to get clarity as to why you made past employment choices. Once you see which beliefs lead you to make those choices, you can review them, changing them, if necessary, to begin attracting a more ideal career.

Day 3 – Getting Clear About What You Want

Hopefully by now you're getting a clear vision of the reasons you ended up in your current and previous jobs, and you're beginning to realize that you have the ability to choose something better.

The question is: What do you want?

This is one of the hardest things to figure out because most of us are not used to choosing what we want. We're used to doing what we have to do, or what others expect of us, or settling for something that is "almost" as good as what we want.

When we try to figure out exactly what we want, our minds go blank. Part of the reason for this is that we're used to thinking in very limited ways. We've been told over and over that our dreams are not practical or realistic. We've told ourselves over and over that we don't have the talent or potential do everything we desire.

So, we shut down our desire for more. Is that what you've done in your life?

I am here to tell you that nothing is impossible. If you can see something in your mind, you can create it in your reality. Whatever type of work you can envision yourself doing is just one possibility of many.

Here's a great way to figure out what type of work would make you happiest: Imagine if you had no limits and could choose any kind of work that you wanted. Salary isn't a concern, so you are free to choose any kind of work you like. What would you choose?

I don't expect you to make a pop decision on this. Take your time and give it the careful consideration it deserves.

Remember, you don't have to know how it will come about! That's another thing that usually stops us cold. Even if we know what we want, we have no idea how to make it happen.

That's the great thing about the Law of Attraction: you don't have to make it happen by yourself! The universe will work with you to make it happen. It will send opportunities your way and shift circumstances so that your dream job becomes a reality.

That doesn't mean you won't have to take some kind of action, because most often you will. But it doesn't have to be hard. It may take some time for you to get used to that, but eventually you'll realize that you just have to do your part, and the universe will do the rest.

Assignment for the Day: Decide the type of work that would make you happiest.

Day 4 – Believing You Can Do Better

Are you feeling clearer about the type of work you want to do? If not, don't worry about it for now. Today's topic will probably help clear out some mental cobwebs.

Limiting beliefs can often be frighteningly powerful in their ability to block us from things we want. What makes them even more tenacious is that they usually exist beneath our conscious level of awareness.

The type of work you've done in the past was probably due to a belief: Either a belief about what you deserved, what you felt you had to do, or what others expected of you.

Even now, your beliefs may be holding you back from deciding what type of work you really want. This usually happens when you know what you'd like to do, but you just can't believe it's possible so you won't entertain the desire.

However, let's start with a belief that's even more basic than these: the belief that you *can* do better now and in the future. No matter how badly you've disliked your previous (or current) job, you have the ability to choose something that makes you feel happy and fulfilled. And you have this choice available at any time. You must believe in this ability before you'll be able to move on to something better. And remember, you don't have to figure it all out on your own. Just believe that it's possible for you to have a job you truly love. The universe will work with you to make it happen.

Not only do I want you to believe that you can do better, I want you to think of your job as a higher calling. Remember, a job is not just a way to make money – it's an expression of you. Only you can do things in your unique way. Only you can contribute to the world with your unique talents and skills. If you don't think your talents and skills are really unique, remember that you bring your own brand of energy and personality to everything you do. Even if someone else is doing a job that is identical to yours, the two of you will contribute your own unique qualities to it.

Think of your work as your vehicle for making a positive change in the world. What would you like your work to say about you after you're gone? How can your work best contribute to others?

When you view your work in this way, it takes on greater meaning and opens the door to many more possibilities!

Assignment for the Day: Today, write down ideas about which aspects of yourself you want your work to reflect.

Day 5 - Follow Your Passion

Hopefully, you've gotten a lot clearer about the type of work that would best suit you. You probably have a better understanding about why you ended up in your current job and the jobs you've held in the past, and you're beginning to expand your beliefs about what is possible for your career. You're off to a great start!

Passion is truly powerful when it comes to the Law of Attraction. Remember that the Law of Attraction responds to your emotional frequency. Feeling passionate about something is one sure way to boost the signal you send to the universe. That includes your work!

When you do something with passion and enthusiasm, you attract wonderful things into your life. Think of passion as a great big magnet that pulls everything good toward you. In the context of your work, that means more money, more satisfaction and raging success!

The trick is to figure out what you feel passionate about and to make sure your dream career is related to it in some way.

What do you feel passionate about? Take a few minutes to jot down some ideas. Think about creative pursuits, hobbies, and any activity you really enjoy. If you could do any of these all day, every day, which would it be? Or would you find a way to combine all of them into one big, passionate pursuit?

Also, be sure to consider your natural strengths and talents, as well as the skills you've developed through experience.

Ideally, the career you have chosen should use these skills while also helping you develop new ones.

It's important to pay attention to the essence of your passions; not necessarily the package they come in.

For example, one of your passions might be art, but you have no desire to be an artist yourself. You simply love art, love looking at art and talking or writing about the arts – which would lead you to a completely different career than actually being an artist yourself.

So, while you're writing down your passions, also consider what it is about them that you love so much. How do they make you feel? Which aspects of them fascinate or thrill you?

Being so specific really helps you to define the essence of what you want to spend most of your time doing. This is helpful because many people start off by saying, "One of my passions is watching soap operas, but no one is going to pay me to do that!"

Ah, but if you dissect exactly what about the soap operas interest you, you might discover that you have a passion for drama, in which case you'd love working at a local theater, or writing for a soap opera magazine – or any other number of possibilities.

See how it works? Identify the essence lurking beneath the activity, and you've got a solid idea of the type of work that would be perfect for you.

Assignment for the Day: Sometimes, we become so focused on lack and the current stresses in our lives, and we forget what evokes passion within us. Do the exercise outlined above to reacquaint yourself with your passions and why they mean so much to you.

Day 6 – Attracting Your Dream Job

By now you know the mindset that led you to the jobs you didn't enjoy and you've spent some time getting clear about the type of work you really want to do. Most importantly, you've identified some strong passions that you'd like your dream job to include.

Now all that remains is to actually attract that dream job! Don't worry; it's quite easy to do – as long as you're willing to be open to the possibilities.

Here are three simple steps to turn your dream job into reality:

1) **Tell the universe what you want.** You already have a strong idea of the type of work that would make you the happiest, but it's helpful to spell it out in detail and to officially submit your request to the universe. However, word it in the present tense like so:

"I now have a fulfilling, fun job at a local art gallery working closely with artists as we prepare their work for exhibition. I earn $50,000 per year and work an average of 30 hours per week."

"I now have a great job as a pet massage therapist. I get to express my love and compassion for animals while contributing to their health and well-being, which makes me feel so fulfilled and inspired. I earn a generous $75 per hour and I get to set my own schedule and work as much or as little as I like."

You get the idea. Be very specific about what type of work you'll be doing, where you'll be doing it, how much it pays, how many hours you work, and anything else that matters to you.

2) **Believe you already have it.** Now begin reciting that statement as often as you can, and really allow yourself to believe you have it, even though it hasn't shown up yet. Be sure to avoid feeling doubtful or anxious about it; just keep believing that it's yours!

Say the statement with absolute confidence and conviction in your voice, as if it were indisputable truth.

At the same time, be sure to avoid contributing negative energy to the process by getting frustrated about your current job. Try your best to detach from what you don't want, and focus more on what you do want. Invest your energy and emotion only in those things you want to multiply.

3) **Finally, have patience.** Don't expect your dream job to show up immediately (though it could). Rather, imagine that the universe is getting the most perfect circumstances together before it delivers your desire. That way, you will have no problem waiting a bit for it because it will be so perfect when it arrives!

Easier said than done, I know. But getting impatient will only prolong your frustration. Just do your best to keep affirming that it's on the way and will arrive at the best possible time.

This attraction process is actually a lot of fun if you allow yourself to enjoy it. The most important thing is to not try to force anything to happen on your own. If you happen to see an opportunity, great! Grab it! But don't try to figure out some big, elaborate scheme just because you don't trust the universe to work with you.

Assignment for the Day: Do one thing to make the attraction process fun. As an example, have a friend do an interview with you. Speaking as though you have your dream job, have your friend ask you questions about what it feels like to have the position, how much it has changed your life, and any advice you would give others who would love to have the same job.

Day 7 – Opening to New Opportunities

Can you feel the sparkle of promise in the air? You've done something really wonderful for yourself and the world by choosing a more fulfilling career path, and good things are going to happen because of it!

You want to be very sure you don't try forcing things to happen on your own. That doesn't mean you can't get the ball rolling by taking action – in fact, I encourage you to! However, it should be action that feels right to you, not just action for the sake of taking action. Make sense?

Here's a good way to tell the difference: Whatever new career path you've decided on, ask yourself if there are any simple steps you can take to move in that direction. Perhaps you could sign up for some evening classes to learn more about the field if it's new to you. Or you might want to consult with someone who is already working in the field you've chosen. Or you might even feel ready to apply for a new job.

Sometimes there won't be any clear actions you can take, and that's okay. In those cases, your job is to simply remain open to the possibilities.

In the days and weeks after you've released your request, you're probably going to notice new opportunities coming your way. It might be a newspaper advertisement related to your new career path, or you'll meet someone who can help, or … The possibilities are endless.

When these opportunities appear, take action! Don't hesitate, don't analyze the situation to death, and don't let fear hold you back – especially if the opportunity doesn't come in a form you would have expected. That's important.

Sometimes you might expect one thing, but it will arrive in a completely roundabout way that you never would have expected. That's why it's important to remain open to all possibilities, not just the way you think it will happen.

Finally, be sure not to discount opportunities that could lead to your dream career.

For example, you might want a career working in a local art gallery like one of the aforementioned examples, but instead you see an advertisement to work with a local artist in his or her studio. That could be the opportunity you need to get your foot in the door of the art world.

Be sure you don't turn away from an opportunity just because it's not exactly what you asked for. Your specific desire could show up later as a result of taking advantage of a slightly different opportunity.

Just stay open to whatever comes your way, and have fun with it! I can't stress that enough. If you're too serious about it, you'll contribute a lesser frequency of energy to the process – and you don't want that.

Assignment for the Day: Affirm to yourself that you are open to any and all opportunities which are waiting to come your way. Allow yourself to keep an open mind to all possibilities (even when they don't seem to readily fit the vision you have).

On a Side Note:

How to Raise Your Frequency

When working with the Law of Attraction, your vibrational frequency is of utmost importance. Vibrate at a low frequency and you'll attract negative events and circumstances; vibrate at a high frequency and you'll attract lots of abundance, love, joy and goodness into your life.

But how do you ensure that you're emitting a high frequency? Below are five easy and fun ways to get into a state of high, positive vibration.

Laugh!

Laughter is one of the most powerful tools in your arsenal against negativity, because it's impossible to emit a low frequency when you're feeling so happy. Invest in some materials that you can count on to inspire laughter whenever you feel the need.

Buy comedies or sitcoms on DVD, get some good joke books or calendars, bookmark some funny Web sites, and make sure to have a good laugh at least once a day.

Get inspired!

Lifting your spirits to a place of inspiration and awe is another great way to raise your frequency, and it's pretty easy to do no matter where you are. Keep inspiring books and movies on hand, and seek out positive people as often as you can. If you have nothing available to help and you need to get into an inspired state, think about something inspiring from your past, or make something up! It doesn't matter if it's real or not, as long as it gets you feeling uplifted and happy.

Get pumped!

This is actually two ideas in one. By "pumped" I'm referring to your mental state first. Think about something that gets you excited and enthusiastic. Bring to mind how you'll feel when you achieve an important goal, or imagine that you're competing in a contest and you're going to win a lot of money or great prizes. The specifics don't really matter; just think of something that makes you feel fired up.

You can also pump up your body through physical activity such as dancing, hiking, aerobics, or any other activity you enjoy. Regardless of the physical activity you select, it will trigger positive emotions and achieve the same results as getting mentally pumped up.

Let your hair down!

Have fun with friends and loved ones as often as you can, or even by yourself if no one else is around. Be silly and have fun, whether you're engaging in creative activities or simply hanging around and relaxing.

Rest!

It's hard to feel positive when you're tired and cranky. Make it your mission to get enough rest on a regular basis, and you'll find that you are also much better capable of keeping your emotions and thoughts in good order.

How to Attract Everything Needed For a Successful Business

Day 1 – What is the Law of Attraction and How Does It Affect My Business?

Over the next seven days we're going to cover some exciting information that should help you to boost your business through the simple process of improving your thoughts, emotions, beliefs and actions.

Remember, the Law of Attraction responds to your thoughts, emotions, and beliefs. Whatever you think, feel and believe the majority of the time will determine the experiences of your life.

Now, you may feel resistant to that idea because you probably don't feel like you're doing anything to attract negative experiences. Who would want to do that? However, understand that most of the time this is done by default. We're not consciously directing our thoughts and emotions toward what we want, but more often toward what we don't want. This makes for some interesting turn of events – and not always good ones.

How does this work in relation to your business?

Your business grows (or doesn't) in relation to the ways you think, feel and believe it will. For example, if you constantly worry about having enough money to keep your business going (and growing), you probably experience plenty of financial snags that cause problems. Even worse, those snags cause you to worry more, which creates more snags, and on it goes!

Another good example: If you find it difficult to build your client base, you probably have a frequent perception of lack, which translates into difficult or nonexistent growth for your business. Even when you're successful at attracting new clients, older clients end up leaving or sales slow down because of other factors.

However, sometimes your influence is not as clear and simple as that. You may believe that you're doing everything you can to make your business succeed, but it's still not working. Sales are slow, clients are jumping ship, and you can't figure out what you're doing wrong.

If that's the case in your business, don't worry! We're going to explore using all of the facets of the Law of Attraction to not only attract new clients, but also to turn your business into the shining success you want it to be.

Once you know how, attracting the success you desire is a simple matter of aligning your thoughts and feelings with what you want, rather than what you don't want.

Assignment for the Day: Give some thought to the things you feel strongly that you don't want. Make a list of the ten "don't wants" you often find yourself focusing on. Can you see how those "don't wants" are persisting because of the energy and attention you are giving them?

Day 2 – Your Business is Your Vessel

Now that you know how the Law of Attraction works to create your experiences, you've probably got an inkling of the reasons your business isn't yet where you want it to be. If you're still trying to figure out where you went wrong, don't worry about it. Over the next few days we're doing to explore exactly how the process works, so you should have a clearer idea soon.

But first, answer this question: Why does your business exist?

Your first response is probably something like, "To make money." That's all well and good, and you're not alone in that expectation. However, have you ever noticed that truly successful businesses often have a bit more substance to them? Yes, their purpose is to make money, but they also contribute something of value to the world, rather than simply "making money."

What does your business contribute to the world?

The reason I ask that question is because I want to shift your perception of your business slightly. Rather than simply seeing it as a cash machine, I want you to see it as a vessel for positive change in the world.

Now, this doesn't have to be some lofty, divine purpose – just something that makes a difference in people's lives.

Once you have an idea of what that purpose is, write it down like the following statement:

"The reason my business exists is so I can _____."

Here are some examples:

> "The reason my business exists is so I can help people save money."

> "The reason my business exists is so I can help people reduce stress."

> "The reason my business exists is so I can help children learn and develop."

Once you've got your purpose written down, put it someplace where you'll see it when you're working. You want to keep that purpose in mind at all times!

In fact, I don't want you to focus on money any more than you absolutely have to in order to run your business. Instead, focus on using your business as a vessel to serve others. Believe me, the money will come – just don't worry about it or obsess over it.

That doesn't mean you can't charge money for your products and services; you absolutely should! In fact, I want to encourage you to re-evaluate how much you're charging, because it may be too little. It's common for many people to undercharge for their products and services because they don't fully believe in the value they are providing to others.

The price you charge for your wares communicates a powerful message to your clients and customers – and to the universe! Charge too little and you appear not to value your own work. Charge too much and you appear to have a streak of greediness. Instead, honestly assess how much value your work provides to others, and price it accordingly.

Then – let the money stuff go! Don't worry about it anymore. Focus only on providing something of value to others.

Assignment for the Day: As instructed, write down the purpose of your business.

Day 3 – Providing Something of Value

Are you feeling more confident about the way your products or services help make others' lives better?

Did you know that everything you create is infused with your energy? Whether you're writing something, creating a work of art or inventing an electronic gadget, you infuse it with your own unique energy brand. That may not sound like a big deal, but it is, simply because the person or people who receive your creation are also receiving the energy you put into it.

Obviously, if you do something carelessly, you'll end up with a lesser quality product or service. That much is clear. But even if the product or service isn't noticeably inferior, your customer or client will not "feel the love," so to speak.

You can probably think of products that you just felt attracted to without knowing why. Something about them just made you feel good! Yet, other products that looked very similar just didn't seem to have the same zing to them.

That's because of the love and attention put into them. I know it sounds a little out there, but people really do pick up on the energy and passion you put into something.

This applies not only to your actual products and services, but also the whole way you run your business. Do you feel passionate and inspired about your business? Or has it become a chore? Do you look forward to sharing your products and services with others, or are you just focusing on trying to make a buck?

Believe me, the differences in energy you emit to the universe with these attitudes are tremendous. And the Law of Attraction responds to the energy and emotion you put out, so it really *does* matter.

Yesterday's assignment of writing a statement to clarify the reason your business exists should help give you the right attitude to attract success. Just be sure you keep that purpose in mind as often as possible. Let it inspire and excite you – and your customers and clients will pick up on that enthusiasm too.

Assignment for the Day: Think of products or services you are strongly attracted to. Write down the reasons why they have made such an impact on you. How could apply the same qualities to your business?

Day 4 – Your Beliefs and Expectations

Are you feeling more inspired and excited about your business now? Hopefully you're gearing up to make another go at it and you're feeling eager to see some positive changes take place.

Today's lesson should help with that because we're exploring your beliefs and expectations as they relate to your business.

First, your expectations.

Do you expect your business to do well? I know you probably hope it will do well, but that's not the same thing. If you spend most of your time worrying that your business won't do well, that means you're expecting it not to do well! I don't think I have to explain how that triggers the Law of Attraction, and what it probably sends in your direction. (Hint: lack, lack, and more lack.)

In order to use the Law of Attraction to create business success, you've got to expect success. How exactly do you do that? By choosing to believe that your business is already successful. You can visualize, meditate, recite affirmations – do whatever it takes to expect good things to come to you.

At all costs, avoid worrying about having enough business, feeling anxious over getting enough clients or customers, and any other negative possibilities you may be tempted to focus on. Just keep expecting good things, knowing that the Law of Attraction is responding to you when you do.

Now, what about your beliefs?

Do you believe in your potential for success? Do you believe in your business, and your own ability to make it successful? Do you believe you deserve the success you desire?

If you don't, you won't allow these things to happen!

You see, your beliefs are like gatekeepers for your perception of reality. Whatever you believe is your truth, and your subconscious mind will not allow you to create something that is contrary to your existing beliefs.

For example, let's say you have been working hard in your business, doing everything you can to attract the success you desire. But deep down, you hold a belief that you don't deserve to be successful and happy. No matter what you do, you won't allow such an outcome to manifest. Instead, you'll find ways to sabotage your efforts.

You've got to be sure you believe that the success you desire is possible, and that you deserve it. One good way to find out is to recite a statement like the following examples and see if they cause any sensations of anxiety or resistance in your body. If you find yourself feeling anxious or jumpy when you say them, you probably don't really believe them.

Assignment for the Day:

Say these statements aloud and pay attention to how you feel:

"I know I deserve to have a successful business."

"I believe in my products (or services)."

"My business has what it takes to be wildly successful."

"I have what it takes to make my business successful."

If those statements do create feelings of resistance within you, you've got to work on changing them. Probably the simplest way to make these changes is to keep reinforcing positive beliefs that will cancel out the negative. It may take time, but with persistence and self-awareness, it will happen.

Day 5 – Promoting Your Products or Services

You've now got a clear understanding of how the Law of Attraction works, you have a new perception of your business as a vessel, you feel confident about the value you provide to others, and you're working on changing limiting beliefs that may have been holding you back. That's great progress!

Today we're going to discuss something that makes many businesspeople cringe: promotion.

What is it about self-promotion that makes many of us shudder? Most often, it's the fear of appearing pushy, greedy or vain. We've been taught to be modest and humble, which is a great thing. That's something to be proud of. However, when our modesty begins to limit our potential for success, we're taking it too far.

In order to attract more business, you've got to toot your own horn a little bit! I know that idea probably doesn't appeal to you, but that's because you're thinking of it a little differently than I am.

When I say, "toot your own horn," you probably imagine that I want you to boast about how great you and your products or services are so you can get more business. It may look that way on the outside, but I want you to go about it from a different perspective.

Rather than boasting for the purposes of getting more business, I want you to think about *sharing* your business with others in an effort to help them.

Yesterday we talked about the power of your beliefs, so I'd like to recap by asking again, do you really believe in your products or services? If you do, if you really see the value they provide to others, why would you want to hold them back from the people who need them?

Ah, promotion looks a bit different from that angle, doesn't it? Now you're focused on other people rather than yourself.

Let me tell you from experience that great things happen when you do this! You are moving from a "getting" to a "giving" perspective, and the universe responds favorably to that.

Assignment for the Day: Every day, for the next 21 days, I want you to commit to doing at least one thing that will put your products or services in front of people who need them. Not in a pushy way, but in a way that helps people see how you can serve them.

Even better, have fun with it! Infuse your promotion efforts with lots of passion and enthusiasm. Remember, people will pick up on that energy and your results will be that much better.

Can you do it? You know you can!

Day 6 – Opening to the Flow of Abundance

Now it's time to ask yourself, are you willing to receive?

Before you answer that, take a minute to consider what the question really means. You may be tempted to answer, "Of course I'm willing to receive! Are you crazy? I'm dying to receive! Send the truckloads of cash my way!"

Unfortunately, you may be resisting abundance and success without even realizing it. It's easy to think you want money and success, but answering yes to any of the following questions may indicate otherwise.

- Do you ever refuse gifts because you feel guilty accepting them?
- Do you ever get flustered by compliments and try to turn the attention elsewhere?
- Do you ever turn away from opportunities because someone else probably needs them more than you do?

These are just simple examples; there are many more situations that reveal the same mindset. If you do things like this, it's a pretty clear sign that you are not open to receiving.

Believe me, when you do things like this, you are sending a very strong signal to the universe! The signal says, "No thanks, I don't deserve it," or "I don't need it," or "I don't feel comfortable accepting it, so go ahead and send it on to someone else."

Here's how to avoid making that mistake:

1) **Every day, affirm that you deserve all good things.** Be grateful for what you have, and affirm that you are open to more. The stronger your self-worth, the more easily you'll be able to accept goodness in all forms, including the money and success that your business attracts.

2) **Express appreciation for everything.** By appreciating the goodness surrounding you, you'll be open to receiving more of it. Do this not only with the gifts and compliments you receive, but also with everything you already have in your life, and everything that will be coming to you soon. Be appreciative, always.

3) **Say aloud as often as you can, "I am open to receiving the abundance and success that is mine."** As you say this statement, allow yourself to feel happy and excited about the wonderful things coming your way. When someone gives you a compliment or gift or when an opportunity drops into your lap, accept it with gratitude!

4) **Be generous.** The more you give to others, the more comfortable you'll feel accepting things for yourself. Be generous with your time, money, advice, support and more.

The whole point of these exercises is to get you into the habit of accepting more than you ask for, rather than turning it away. The more you do that, the more the universe will send your way!

Assignment for the Day: Today, begin to create a morning ritual devoted to opening the flow of abundance. Create a ritual you will do each day that will include whatever practices hold the most power for you. Make sure your practices include visualizing, writing down your desires, and giving thanks for all that has manifested already.

Day 7 – Allowing Success and Growth

Allowing is actually a state of being, rather than doing. It means being open to the goodness the universe is sending your way without trying to force things to happen in the way and at the time you want them to.

When most of us want something, we tend to try to hurry it along so we can have it immediately. In the context of business, you may be rushing to make more money, make your business grow, or achieve other goals.

By doing that, you are affirming to the universe that things are not okay as they are right now. Maybe that's exactly how you feel. The problem is that when you feel that things are not okay, the universe will send you more "not okay." You don't want that!

Allowing means shifting into the mindset of knowing that the universe is working with you and everything is happening in its own perfect time. It means relaxing and enjoying the ride, rather than racing to the finish line.

Remember, this imparts a fantastic quality of energy to your business! You can focus more on your passion and enjoyment of your day-to-day business activities, rather than focusing only on some distant destination.

The best and simplest way to "allow" the success you desire is by thinking, feeling and acting as if it were already here. Rather than forcing yourself to work too hard, or getting panicky about not having enough business, pretend you have plenty of business and you can afford to take time off.

Assignment for the Day:

Focus more on the enjoyment you get from your work, rather than the amount of money it yields. Focus more on what you can do for others, rather than what their purchases will do for you.

When you do this, you activate the Law of Attraction in very beneficial ways. The more you focus on goodness and abundance, the more goodness and abundance can come your way.

CORE CONCEPTS:

Three Steps to Activate the Law of Attraction

To use the Law of Attraction deliberately, you'll use a simple, three-step process:

1) Ask.
2) Believe.
3) Receive.

Wow, that does sound simple, doesn't it? But is it really as easy as saying, "Please give me a million dollars," believing you'll get it, and then having it manifest before you in a puff of smoke? Not quite. While you may experience plenty of "miracles" and amazing moments as you learn to work with the Law of Attraction, most often it won't be quite that cut and dried.

Ask

Asking the universe for what you want is not quite the same as simply verbalizing something out loud in question form. Before you even do that, it's vital to get very clear about what you want.

Most of us are not clear at all about what we want. We just know we're not happy and we want things to be better. But the Law of Attraction needs a little more information than that. Imagine walking into a restaurant and saying to the server, "Bring me something good to eat." What are the odds that you'll get something you actually want?

When you ask the universe for something, you need to be specific, just like you would in a restaurant. What exactly do you want?

Take a few minutes right now and jot down things or situations you'd like to attract into your life. It could be a better job, more money, a loving relationship, better health, or anything else. Put as much detail as you can into the descriptions of these things. Don't just say, "I want a better paying job." Say, "I want a fun job as a public relations assistant in the city of _____, earning $80,000 per year and working approximately 35 hours per week."

Once you've got a crystal clear idea of what you want, it's time to ask for it.

Writing down your desires is an excellent way to clarify them and to "deliver" them to the universe. There are other options too, however:

- **Create a Vision Board.** You've probably seen these before. If not, they consist of some type of board or poster upon which you stick magazine photos and images of things you want to attract into your life, such as a new car, your dream home, soul mate, and so on. Images are helpful because you can see clearly what you're asking for, rather than trying to remember to write down every last detail.

- **Say it out loud.** You may find it helpful to make this a somewhat "ceremonial" activity, rather than just blurting it out any old time. Consider having a meditation session where you take a few minutes to quiet your mind, then speak out loud to the universe as if you were talking to a good friend. You might say something like, "Dear universe, I am finally getting clear on what I want to bring into my life, and I ask that you help me to do so. Here's what I'd love to have happen: _____ (state your desires in full detail). Please help me create these experiences by providing the opportunities and insight I need to transform my life." The actual words don't matter; just the sentiment and intention you are conveying.

- **Visualize it.** Visualization is a great tool to help attract better experiences into your life. It works better if you do it on a regular basis, rather than just once. Set aside 10 to 15 minutes to visualize daily. Simply relax and quiet your mind, then call up an image of something you want. See it in full detail in your mind's eye, and allow yourself to feel like you would if you already had it. Bring up feelings of excitement, joy, happiness, contentment, love – or any emotion that matches what you're trying to attract.

- **Affirm it.** Affirmations are also helpful tools because they keep your thoughts and emotions flowing in a positive direction. Affirmations also work best if you recite them frequently, and they should be worded in a way that makes them more believable. Rather than saying, "I am now wealthy," try something closer to this, "My wealth and abundance are increasing every day." The first example would likely be blocked by your subconscious mind because you know it's not true. However, the second example makes it sound a little more possible, so your mind will be more receptive to it.

It doesn't really matter how you choose to get your request across to the universe, so do what feels most natural to you.

You may be wondering if it's necessary to keep asking until your desire has manifested, or if once is enough. For the most part, no, you don't have to keep asking.

Keeping your desires strong in your mind can help you stay in the right frequency to attract them. Still, using the techniques above on a regular basis is a good idea. You don't have to nag or beg the universe – just keep affirming and knowing that your desires are being formed.

Believe

Once you've asked for what you want, you have to work on believing you can, and will, have it. This can be tricky because limiting beliefs often prevents what you want from forming in your life.

Probably the two most common limiting beliefs are these:

• **Not believing you deserve to have what you want.** Low self-esteem is one mindset that can create big problems when working with the Law of Attraction. Logically you may know that you're a good person and you deserve to have a happier life, but deep down inside you may not really feel that way.

You'll know when you have a belief like this because you'll probably feel anxious or uncomfortable about accepting good things into your life. On one hand, you know you deserve to have something, but, on the other hand, you feel like it would be too good to be true if it did happen. You might experience moments of guilt, doubt or hesitation when you think about having more abundance and goodness in your life, because there are others who are suffering that could use it more than you could.

In order to overcome these beliefs, you'll need to work on boosting your self-esteem and affirm that you really do deserve to have the things you want. You'll need to release your perception of a limited universe, and remember that everyone has the power to attract great things into his or her life just like you do.

Remember, the happier and more abundant you are, the more you'll be able to contribute to the world, financially and otherwise.

• **Not believing it's possible to have what you want.** This is another big limiting belief. You probably hope that it's possible to have what you want, but do you really believe it is possible?

It's tough to foster this level of faith and conviction when you're first learning to work with the Law of Attraction because you don't yet have any "evidence" that it really works. As time goes on and you begin to see results in your own life, you'll eventually come to believe that anything is possible. But in the meantime, you may need to work a little harder at choosing to believe it.

Not believing that something is possible is only one side of this limiting belief; the other side involves believing that something has to happen in a specific way for it to be possible. For example, if you've asked for a large sum of money, you may think that winning the lottery is the only way such a large sum could come to you. If you hold that as a belief, however, you'll be blocking all other possibilities from manifesting!

To overcome this limiting mindset, remember that the universe has unlimited resources at its disposal. Just because you can't see any other way doesn't mean the universe can't! Do your best to stay open to the possibilities – even the ones you can't imagine right now.

Believing is often the most challenging of this three-step process because most of us are so used to not believing. We're used to doubting, fearing, resisting, and struggling to get what we want. That very attitude, however, is what keeps us from attracting what we want.

One good way to turn your beliefs away from lack and toward abundance is by saying an affirmation like this multiple times a day:

"I always have more than enough _____ . . ."

Examples:

"I always have more than enough money for everything I need."

"I always have more than enough time to take care of my obligations."

"I always have more than enough love in my life."

"I always have more than enough of anything I need."

Over time, this type of affirmation will help you form a solid belief that there is no such thing as lack or limitation, and you simply need to keep reinforcing it in your mind until it "sets." The longer and more frequently you reinforce this type of belief, the stronger and more powerful it gets!

Receive

Alright! Now you've asked for what you want, you are working on believing that it's possible and you deserve it, and now you're ready to receive. What this means is that you have to be open to receive. You might think you're already open to receive, but it may not mean what you think it does.

Being open to receive means letting go of any emotional attachment you have to your desires coming true. It means not getting impatient or frustrated when they don't show up right away, worrying and obsessing about when they might show up, or trying to force the process to hurry along.

If you're doing any of those things, you are not open to receive! Being open to receive means being in a state of "allowing" – not grasping, begging, desperation, or fear. That's not always easy to achieve, but it's necessary if you want to use the Law of Attraction to its fullest potential.

In order to fully receive and have your desire manifest, you need to let go of any "need" for it. Instead, simply allow the universe to work on your behalf.

One of the easiest ways to allow is to sit or lie quietly in meditation one or more times per day. It can be for short periods of time, such as 10 to 20 minutes. During that time, simply clear your mind of all worries, doubts, fears and frustrations and focus on opening to the natural flow of abundance from the universe. Don't think about anything in particular or try to make something happen, just focus on opening yourself to all the abundance that is rightfully yours.

If you wish, you can visualize a stream of light flowing from the universe through your body and mind, or you can simply focus on feeling happy. When you do this, you are automatically in a state of allowing!

Inspired Action

Sometimes the universe will also inspire you to take a specific action to help your desire come forth into physical reality. You might get offered a job, or feel an urge to call an old friend, or get an idea to research specific opportunities relating to something you want.

There are unlimited ways it can all come together, so be sure to stay open to any opportunities that might come along.

If you don't feel a nudge to take action right away, there are two things you can do:

1) **Wait and watch for the universe to lead you in a certain direction.** Inspired actions can pop up at any time, so if you don't get one right away, keep aware and wait and see if one comes along later.

2) **Think about actions you can take on your own.** With any goal or aspiration, there are usually a few simple steps that you could take to begin moving toward what you want. Rather than waiting for the universe to help, do what you can to get things moving in the direction you want to go. You don't have to take on the whole thing yourself or make your actions very difficult or strenuous – in fact, if you do that, you're not allowing the universe to work with you! But show your willingness to open as many "gateways" for abundance as you can, and the universe will do the same by sending increased opportunities.

CONCLUSION

Other Pieces of the Puzzle

For most of your life, you have probably been operating on autopilot with the things you've attracted. You may not be used to consciously directing your thoughts, emotions and beliefs, so you attract many things by default.

Use the following information and exercises to help you gain control of your mental and emotional states so you can become a more conscious creator.

Thoughts

Learning how to direct your thoughts in a more positive direction is vital to mastering the Law of Attraction. Your thoughts alone don't really attract anything on their own. But, they do govern your emotions, which do attract plenty. Take a moment and look at the list of adjectives below and consider whether any of them could be used to describe your usual state of mind:

- Pessimistic
- Frustrated
- Angry
- Impatient
- Doubtful
- Anxious
- Fearful
- Stressed
- Overwhelmed

- Sad
- Depressed
- Cynical
- Skeptical

If you emit these types of thoughts on a regular basis, you are putting forth a negative signal to the universe and likely attracting back corresponding situations and events.

To turn it around, begin working on the quality of your thoughts right away. Make an effort to think more positively, be more optimistic, and be happy as often as you can. When you catch yourself getting impatient or frustrated with your current circumstances, or doubting that things will work out for the best, immediately begin turning those thoughts around!

This may not be an easy habit to change, especially if you've been thinking negatively for a long time. The more you work at it, however, the easier it will get to keep it going.

There are basically two ways to work on improving your thoughts:

1) **When you notice yourself thinking negatively, change your frame of mind.** As described above, you'll have to work on "putting out fires" when you notice negative thoughts taking control of your mind. It will take a bit of willpower and focus to turn them back to a positive direction, but there are things that can help, like reading or watching something funny on television, doing things you enjoy, or spending time with loved ones and friends.

2) **Be more proactive in your positive thinking, every day.** Rather than waiting for negative thoughts to pop up in your mind, get into the habit of purposely feeding your mind positive thoughts daily. Read uplifting and inspiring books, write and recite affirmations, watch inspiring movies, and hang around with positive, successful people as often as you can. This type of habit can affect profound change in you, regardless of how negative your thoughts were before!

Emotions

Improving the quality of your thoughts will go a long way in boosting your emotional state, because positive thoughts trigger positive feelings, which will automatically change the frequency of your signal. However, you can also take a more active role in emitting positive emotions by simply choosing to feel happy!

Try to accompany your happiness with feelings of being grateful, joyful, passionate, hopeful, and content with your life exactly as it is right now. This may prove challenging, too, because most of us are used to complaining about the negative things in our lives rather than focusing on the positive side.

If you typically do the same thing, start a new practice of purposely bringing up positive emotions as often as possible. If you can't do it on command, consider using activities to help stimulate your emotions, like those described to improve your thoughts. Just a few minutes focusing on something more positive can get your emotions flowing in positive and powerful ways.

Your emotions can also serve as an excellent warning system when your thoughts start to take a nosedive into the negative. As soon as you realize you're feeling sad, frustrated, angry, resentful or fearful, it's a sure sign that you've been thinking negative thoughts! Your thoughts trigger your emotions, so keep on the lookout for any seemingly random negative emotions and take steps to improve your line of thought right away.

Expectations

Do you often catch yourself expecting the worst? Do you say things like, "This is going to be a bad day," or "I know it's not going to work out the way I hope"? If so, you are holding negative expectations, which will affect your results with the Law of Attraction.

An expectation is a type of belief, and the Law of Attraction uses your beliefs to determine what you will accept or resist! By uttering a negative expectation like the examples above, you are in effect telling the universe: "This is what I choose to experience." Even though that's not what you intend to choose, it's still what you're communicating with your thoughts, feelings and beliefs.

To turn this around, you've got to start expecting the best in all situations. Once again, it will probably take a bit of willpower and persistence to make it a true habit, but it becomes easier as you go along.

If you catch yourself thinking or verbalizing a negative expectation, turn it around to something like, "Wait, that's just a perception. What I choose to believe is that somehow, someway it will all work out perfectly."

Acknowledging that the expectation is simply a perception makes it more believable because you're not going against what you perceive to be "true." Rather, you are choosing what you want to be true.

What Not to Do

In addition to incorporating these new habits into your life, you will also want to make a concentrated effort *not* to do those things that will lower the frequency of your vibration. If you allow the frequency to be lowered, you will delay the arrival of the things you want. Some things that can make this happen include the following:

1. Thinking or Feeling Negatively

We've already discussed the importance of improving the quality of your thoughts and emotions, but old habits may die hard. You may find yourself slipping back into old ways of thinking and feeling when something in your surroundings triggers you. You won't be able to avoid all negative thoughts and emotions. But if you try very hard to stay positive as much as possible, you'll shift the balance and be sure you're emitting more positive vibrations than negative ones. Over time, that begins to add up and you'll find your circumstances shifting to match.

2. Being Impatient

It's hard not to feel impatient when you're unhappy with your circumstances and you're wishing for something better but it's not showing up yet. But by getting impatient, you are simply affirming the lack of what you want to the universe! You are saying, "I don't have this, and I'm unhappy about it." The universe sends you more "not having" and unhappiness.

Try your hardest to stay in a place of allowing and knowing that your desires are on the way and they will arrive at exactly the right time. The more effectively you can do this, the more quickly your desires will show up.

3. Doubting That It Works

Remember, the Law of Attraction responds to your thoughts, emotions and beliefs. If you get caught up in doubt that it works, you'll be expressing a belief that it doesn't work, so it won't work! As difficult as it may be, you've got to choose to believe that it works, even if you haven't seen any proof in your life yet.

If you have to, read stories about other people who have experienced success with it. Talk with other people who have mastered the techniques and keep reinforcing your belief as often as possible. Eventually, you'll develop a solid belief.

4. Focusing on What You Don't Want

Most of us are so used to doing this that it may take some strong effort to pull out of the habit. As you go about your daily activities, be on the lookout for signals that you're focusing on what you don't want, such as complaining or obsessing about negative situations or focusing on lack in any way.

When you catch yourself doing this, you'll have to switch your focus back to something you do want, and get into a positive state of emotion about it. Here's an example so you can see how it works:

Imagine that you've got a lot of debt and you're barely able to pay your bills each month, so you find that you keep worrying anxiously about having enough money. Lack is what you don't want, and the more you keep focusing on it with negative emotions like anxiety and fear, the more of it you're going to attract!

Instead, you need to somehow start focusing more on abundance. You can do that by feeling grateful for all the abundance you do have, or by affirming that you always have more than enough money to pay your bills, or even by visualizing more money flowing into your life.

Remove your focus from what you don't want, and place it squarely on what you do want, and you'll begin to attract more of it!

What To DEFINITELY Do!

Enough of the negative stuff – let's end this book on a positive, powerful note. Below, you'll find a simple explanation of everything you should do as often as possible if you really want to get the Law of Attraction working more positively in your life.

Dance, laugh, sing, create and enjoy every aspect of your life! Do the work you love, contribute something of value to the world, affirm abundance as often as possible, and be generous with your time, money and resources.

Love others with compassion and joy, treat yourself with respect and tenderness, and keep your dreams and hopes alive and strong. Believe with all of your heart that you have the power to create your life and make it whatever you want it to be.

Affirm constantly that you are a beautiful, miraculous child of the universe that deserves to have all of the desires of your heart. Believe and know that they are on their way to you, and do your best to help other people get what they want too!

Turn every moment of your life into an expression of absolute joy, happiness, harmony, love, abundance and gratitude.

When you do these things, the signal you are sending to the universe becomes so strong and focused that you won't be able to help but attract amazing and wonderful things to yourself.

Remember that it's a process. You are learning how to become a different person than you used to be. You used to be someone who was unaware of the immense power you have to change your world. You are awakening now, but give yourself time and room to grow into the knowledge fully.

One of the best things about awakening to your true power is the chance to take full responsibility for your life. Though it may not always be comfortable to know that you're attracting things you don't want, there is empowerment in knowing that you can choose something better at any time!

If you stumble, fall, or backslide into old habits, don't lose hope. Simply pick yourself up and get back on track again. It will take practice, persistence and patience at the beginning, but one day you'll realize that it's become a more automatic process and you don't have to work so hard at it anymore. That's when you'll really be able to see what you're capable of!

In the meantime, take your time, be patient with yourself and keep a constant expectation of awe. Expect to see miracles and wondrous things wherever you go. Let the universe surprise and delight you and, before you know it, you'll have opened a whole new world of possibility for yourself – and there won't be anything you can't do.

*I hope that you'll visit me online at **BoldThoughts.com** to share your successes as well as ask any questions that come up.*

BONUS SECTION:

WHAT TO DO WHEN THE LAW OF ATTRACTION ISN'T WORKING

How to Dissolve Blockages and Clear the Way to the Life of Your Dreams

There is no greater gift than the realization that you and you alone have the power to create the life of your dreams, and an understanding of the Law of Attraction has given that gift to millions of people through many centuries.

However, there are many people who still cannot seem to get this mysterious law working for them. Are you one of those people? If so, this is going to be one of the most helpful and life-changing guides you will ever read.

Believe it or not, when most people struggle to get the Law of Attraction working for them, they are usually making some minor common mistakes that can be resolved quickly and easily with just a little bit of focused attention.

I am going to highlight these common mistakes and reveal some simple steps to help you turn them around and start experiencing massive success with the Law of Attraction – no matter how many times you have tried and "failed" before.

Let's start with a brief overview of the steps required to manifest what you want:

Changing Your Thoughts

First and foremost, in order to attract something into your life, you need to consistently focus on it. This can be accomplished in different ways, many of which you have probably tried already.

Visualization, affirmations, scripting, vision boards – all of these activities help keep your thoughts focused on the things you want to attract into your life.

In addition to these activities, it is also important to keep your thoughts aligned with what you want during the course of your day – not just for 15 or 20 minutes while you are visualizing.

That means deliberately turning your thoughts in a more positive direction when you notice you are focusing on negativity, lack or struggle. Ideally, you want to consistently train your brain to focus on the things you WANT, rather than the things you DON'T WANT.

Like:

- Focusing on abundance rather than lack
- Focusing on happiness rather than anger
- Focusing on well-being rather than illness
- Focusing on love rather than loneliness

Balancing Your Emotional Responses

Beyond changing your thoughts from negative to positive, your emotional responses also need to be balanced with your new, more positive thought patterns. For example, you can't spend all day focusing on joy and abundance and then blow an emotional fuse when someone cuts you off in traffic. Learning better ways to cope with stress and frustration will go a long way in helping to keep your emotions balanced.

Even better, much of this emotional balancing will happen automatically as you continuously choose better thoughts. Since your thoughts trigger your emotional responses, you will notice that purposely directing your thoughts in more positive ways naturally helps you feel calmer and happier.

Improving Your Physical Surroundings

Another important step is making consistent changes in your surrounding environment to better match your improving mind-set. For example, you may find yourself feeling uncomfortable with people who are often angry and complain a lot, since you are trying to focus more on the positive. As a result, you may gravitate toward successful, confident, motivated people rather than those who think of themselves as "victims."

As your mind-set continues to improve and expand, you may also feel a desire to move to a better area, change careers, and even create entirely new social activities.

Changing Limiting Beliefs

As you begin to focus on better thoughts, improve your emotional responses and make more positive changes in your life, you will undoubtedly bump up against a few limiting beliefs that need to be cleared before you can continue moving forward.

You may discover that you have a deeply ingrained belief that you don't deserve to be happy, loved, wealthy, or healthy. You may believe that good things can only come to you through hard work and sacrifice. You may believe that your opportunities to become successful are extremely limited – or don't exist at all.

Whatever limiting beliefs you uncover, changing them is as simple as realizing that they are illusions. For example, if you recognize a belief that you don't deserve to be happy, consider why you believe that to be true. Did someone in your life communicate that to you? And do you want to continue to believe it?

Affirm that you have the power to believe whatever you want about yourself and your life – and you can *choose* better beliefs by simply repeating them to yourself consistently.

Affirmations such as these can be powerful:

- "I do deserve to be happy, healthy and wealthy."
- "I choose to believe in my own worthiness."
- "I now release the belief that I'm not good enough."
- "I love and accept myself exactly as I am right now."

Making Gratitude a Way of Life

Finally, in order to attract anything into your life, you need to be mentally and emotionally aligned with receiving it. When it comes to good things like abundance and prosperity, success, healthy relationships and physical well-being, it's important to keep yourself in a state of "allowing" so your goodness can be delivered. And an attitude of gratitude is one of the simplest and most powerful ways to do that.

Every time you say "thank you" for something you have or appreciate, you are communicating a powerful message to the universe to keep sending more and more things to appreciate and feel thankful for. That includes everything you have been visualizing, affirming and dreaming about all your life.

But it's not enough to just say the words "thank you." You need to actually *feel* that warm, wonderful essence of gratitude and appreciation flowing through your body as you reflect on the things you are grateful for. Every time you do this, you create a clear channel for everything you desire to come flooding into your life.

Been There, Done That!

You are probably familiar with all the aforementioned steps, and perhaps you've been doing all of them consistently for weeks – or even months – but still aren't getting any results. Does that mean that the Law of Attraction just won't work for you?

Absolutely not!

What it does mean is that you are probably doing one or more small things that are keeping your desires from manifesting – or you are neglecting to do one or more small things that would help bring them into physical reality.

More often than not, when people feel stuck, a tiny adjustment is all that's needed to open the floodgates and get things moving forward again. But there are some surprisingly easy changes you can make to finally move beyond inertia and make some real progress with the Law of Attraction.

Identify the True Essence of Your Desire

First, it is extremely important to get very clear on the essence of what you are trying to achieve. Very often people choose a goal that they believe will make them feel a certain way, but they're not interested in the goal itself – just the feeling they believe will result from it.

For example, perhaps you have been trying with all of your might to build a business that will pay a substantial passive income so you can have more time to spend with your family and do things you enjoy. The essence of your desire is to have plenty of money and freedom so you can live life on your own terms. But you may have chosen a business model that does not give you that feeling of freedom and fun, so you resist taking the steps that would create the passive income you want. Do you see the problem here? You want the feeling of fun, freedom and abundance – but the method you have chosen to create it is not in alignment with such feelings.

A much better approach would be to focus on the feeling you want to create (fun, freedom, abundance) and ask the universe to show you the best way to achieve it. When you do this, you instantly dissolve your inner conflict and create many more opportunities to create exactly what you want.

Stop Noticing That It Isn't Here Yet

One of the more common obstacles that many people encounter is the temptation to keep splitting their focus between what they want and what they don't want. For example, they will spend a few minutes each day focusing on abundance, and then spend the rest of their day focusing on how little money they actually have, or feeling stressed because they have too many bills or that they can't do the things they want to do because they can't afford them. Unfortunately, all this does is send mixed signals to the universe so nothing can change!

As difficult as it sounds, you really need to force your thoughts away from the things you don't want to keep replicating in your physical reality, and focus them solely on the things you *do* want to expand. One good way to do this is to see every moment as an opportunity to choose a better focus. When you notice that you are focusing on a lack of money (or anything else you want), grasp that opportunity to deliberately choose better thoughts.

Say to yourself, "All right, I may not yet have everything I want, but I do believe it's coming soon. I know that this perception of lack is only temporary. I know that someday soon I will have plenty of money and it's going to be so much fun!" The words you use don't matter – only the fact that you are choosing to focus on something you want, rather than something you don't want.

The catch: you need to do this consistently, day after day, before you will start to see consistent results from it. But it works like a charm, so give it your full attention!

Don't Try to Do It All Yourself

One of the things that often creates a lot of frustration is trying to do everything yourself. You conceive a desire, spend time visualizing it and building up your excitement about it – and then immediately rush out and start taking massive action to get the ball rolling. Essentially what you are doing is trying to "make things happen" but more often than not this ends up creating a lot of resistance.

Taking action is not a bad thing, except when it is done because you don't trust the universe to work on your behalf, or because you are too impatient to wait for results to come in their own good time.

Consider both of these points carefully because they communicate a powerful message to the universe about doubt and distrust. When you shove the universe out of the way, you are not using the Law of Attraction – you are using the "law of physical action" – otherwise known as the "law of working your tail off to get what you want."

If you have been doing this, you will find it much easier to step back and stop trying to take on everything yourself for a while. Instead, communicate what you want and be willing to release it to the universe. Within a few days to a few weeks you will most likely find that you'll receive a nudge or hunch about something specific you can do to help move things along – and this type of inspired action is always much easier than actions that attempt to force things to happen.

Consult Your Inner Guidance

You don't always have to wait for inspired guidance to come to you spontaneously, either! Get into the habit of sitting quietly for a few minutes each day, and ask your inner wisdom (also known as your inner self, higher self, inner being; whatever you wish to call it) whether there is anything specific you can do to help manifest your desires.

An example question might be: "What can I do to increase my likelihood of getting a higher paying job?"

Listen quietly for an answer for a few minutes. Pay attention to any mental images, feelings, hunches or "gut feelings" you receive, and trust your intuition if you decide to act on them.

If no answers seem to come to you immediately, let go of the situation for now and wait to see what happens. An inspired idea may jump out at you when you least expect it.

You can also ask for guidance on specific action steps you are considering: "Would it be a good idea to start this business with John?" You may receive a clear yes-or-no feeling, or it may be a subtler leaning toward one choice or another.

Doing this daily with every major decision in your life can be a powerful exercise because essentially you are making it clear to the universe that you intend to be a co-creator with it. Before long, you'll start receiving many more inspired ideas and insights for creating a truly joyful, successful life – quickly, easily, and without struggle or confusion.

Trust the Universe

Sometimes people have a hard time trusting the universe, and this could potentially be a blockage for you too. Do you ever have the feeling that the universe is punishing you, withholding the things you want, or deliberately making life harder for you?

This is often the result of conditioning that makes you believe that "God" (or "Universe" or any other term you use to refer to a higher spiritual power) is judgmental, angry or unkind. If you see the universe in this way, you may still be carrying a belief that your abundance is dependent upon being good enough to please the "powers that be" – and if you don't consider yourself good enough, you may hold yourself back from allowing it in.

But what if you were to develop a belief that the universe is completely loving and kind? What if you were to know deep inside that you are worthy of everything you want – and the universe not only wants you to have it but is eager to help you get it as quickly as possible?

Changing your perception in this way can dissolve inner conflict caused by feelings of unworthiness and/or distrust of the universe.

One good way to begin changing this belief is to keep saying repeatedly, "I trust you completely, universe. I know you are working on my behalf and you will let me know if there is anything I can do to help move things along. Otherwise I am turning this situation over to you and I know you'll make it happen in the best possible way."

You may not really believe what you are saying the first few times you try this, but if you keep saying it anyway little by little you will start to believe it. And then the universe begins responding back to you as if that were indeed "true." It only becomes your truth when you believe it!

Do You REALLY Want It?

Sometimes when we set big goals, we are also a little bit afraid of them at the same time. It's not that we don't want to have them – but part of us might feel uncertain about our ability to handle the results, or we may have a slight doubt that we deserve them, or any other number of uncomfortable fears.

For example, if you were to ask the universe for a large sum of money, you may feel very excited about having it, but at the same time part of you might worry that your relatives would demand money from you, or stop speaking to you if you didn't comply with their wishes. Or perhaps you have a strong desire to lose weight, but part of you may feel scared about being slender because you may attract unwanted attention or propositions that you're not prepared to handle. Or you may be using your excess pounds as an excuse not to pursue some bigger dreams, and if the weight disappeared so would your excuses.

There are endless reasons why you may be partially resisting the manifestation of your desires, but clearing these inner conflicts is pretty easy to do.

Here's an eye-opening exercise:

Write on a sheet of paper: "If I were to have _____, I'm afraid it would cause a problem with _____" Fill in the first blank with your desire, and the second blank with whatever fears or problems you think could result if you were to achieve it.

Example: "If I were to have a lot of money, I'm afraid it would cause a problem with my friends because they would feel uncomfortable around me, or they might expect me to pay for all of our activities, or bail them out of their own financial problems."

Once you have identified one or more fears, write a few solutions like this:

"If _____ did happen, I would respond this way: _____." Then come up with ways that you could cope with the problem if it occurred.

Examples:

"If my family and friends did become demanding about money, I would give them $_____ and make it clear that that was all I could do for them."

"If my family and friends did start to treat me differently, I would show them with my actions that I'm still the same person they know and love."

You may need to do this exercise several times before you start to feel more confident – but the more you do it you will be reinforcing your own ability to handle anything that happens. This builds your confidence and dissolves your inner resistance – and your desire is then free to manifest!

Dig Up Limiting Beliefs

Similar to hidden fears, you may also have some ingrained beliefs that could be holding back your desires. An easy way to find out for sure is to say statements similar to these:

> "I know I deserve to be wealthy."
> "I am going to lose this weight for good."
> "I trust that the universe will help me."

Right after you say one of these statements, pay close attention to how you feel. Do you notice any sensations of discomfort, doubt, disbelief, fear or other negative emotion? If so, there's a very good possibility that you don't really believe what you are saying. If you explore that feeling a little more, you will begin to understand why.

Here's an example so you can see how it works. Imagine you just recited the statement, "I know I deserve to be wealthy" and you felt a wave of doubt or discomfort flow through you. As you tuned into that discomfort you might become aware of random thoughts like these running through your mind: "But no one in my family has ever been wealthy. None of them even graduated high school except for me. How can I become wealthy if they couldn't do it either?"

Bingo! You have just identified a very real limiting belief that has the power to hold back your wealth! Now you can begin working on reversing this limiting belief by speaking or writing statements that will override it.

Something like these might work well: "My family would be so proud of me, just like they were proud of me for graduating high school. It's my duty to be successful because I know they would want that for me. Becoming wealthy is easy if I share my gifts with the world."

Simply work on changing the limiting beliefs you uncover, and before long you will notice that those "buts" no longer come up when you think about the things you want.

Prepare for the Arrival of Your Desires

One of the surest ways to gauge your level of belief is to pay attention to how prepared you are to receive your desires. Saying that you believe they are on the way is one thing; taking action that confirms your belief is another thing entirely!

If you truly believed that you were going to meet your soul mate any day, how would you prepare for such a meeting? Would you have your hair cut and styled? Would you free up some time in your schedule to allow for fun outings? Would you be more proactive about releasing past relationships? Would you do everything you could to make room for this person in your life?

It works the same way whether you are asking for a new relationship, better health, more money, a different career or anything else. Taking physical action to prepare for it conveys a powerful message to the universe that you fully expect to receive it soon. And that level of belief is extremely persuasive when it comes to the Law of Attraction!

However, most of us do the opposite; we hold back, waiting, waiting, waiting, sure that it will come someday, but not any time soon. What message does that send?

Starting now, act as if your desire were going to arrive at any moment, and do what you can to create a space for it in every area of your life.

Surrender to a Broader Perspective

For every desire you have, the universe has billions of possible ways to deliver it to you. Yes, BILLIONS.

Most of us, however, tend to doubt that the universe really knows what we want and worry that we might get something else instead – or nothing at all. As a result, we try to control every little detail of our desires manifesting – and usually end up creating delays or other obstacles.

One of the most powerful things you can do with every one of your desires is to completely surrender them to the universe and be very deliberate about doing so. You can even say out loud, "Here is what I want in full detail," (explain the situations clearly here) "and now I am turning this over to you and letting go of it."

Then, follow through by *truly letting go* – never once doubting that it will be delivered, never once trying to control the outcome, never once wondering where it is and when it will come.

Doing this is one of the fastest ways to receive your desires because you are not closing the door on any possibilities, which means the universe doesn't have to try to squeeze around any block of resistance in order to get something good to you. It simply chooses the easiest, fastest way and sends it boomeranging right back to you!

And most of the time you will realize that you don't care so much about how it comes, or what form it takes, or any of those details, simply because the feeling it gives you is exactly what you wanted anyway.

Surrender fully to a higher wisdom and watch how quickly your life begins to transform.

Bringing Your Future Joy Into Your Now

Another common blockage occurs when you keep holding back on happiness until your desires are manifested. It may seem like you would feel happier once you have more money, a better job, the love of your life, the dream house or whatever else you are working toward – but you cannot keep radiating thoughts and feelings of dissatisfaction now and attract something that makes you feel happy and satisfied in the future. The two frequencies are completely different and cannot coexist.

On the other hand, when you begin feeling happy and satisfied *now*, you are investing in future manifestations that also make you feel happy and satisfied later.

Now for the million-dollar question: How can you feel happy and satisfied when you don't yet have what you want, and are still experiencing things that you don't want?

Believe it or not, it's as simple as finding just one thing to focus on that makes you feel happy right now. As I mentioned earlier, you could focus on feeling grateful for everything in your life. Or you could focus on the love you feel for your children, pets, spouse, or friends. Or you could think about a fond memory that fills you with love and laughter. Or you can imagine how great it will be when you have received the things you want.

Whatever you focus on, understand that it doesn't even have to be related to the things you're trying to attract! You could feel happy about a gorgeous sunrise and attract a pay raise at work. You could feel grateful for your home and attract improved family relationships. All of it is interconnected.

However you choose to do it, make it your mission to feel joyful, happy, grateful, or satisfied as often as you can. The more you do it, the more you will attract experiences that make you feel exactly like that.

Patience, Trust and Practice

Hopefully by now you can see that working deliberately with the Law of Attraction is easy – even if you do need to tweak your approach a little bit here and there.

Even though it may seem like you'll never get where you want to be, you need to know that all of the wonderful things you desire are just waiting to come flooding into your life.

All of the time and energy you have spent focusing on these things has not been in vain. You have generated a lot of energy and intention and that is enough to begin pulling your desired outcomes toward you.

It is never too late to clarify and hone your desires, and it is never too late to ask the universe to co-create them with you. It is never too late to learn a new technique, release limiting beliefs and start living the life you truly deserve.

You already have all of the tools you need to create anything and everything you desire. The only thing missing is a rock-solid belief in yourself and the courage to try once more.

Begin inching open those floodgates to clear the way for the good stuff to flow in. Take it a step at a time, trust the process, trust the universe, and know that no matter how far you may have seemed to veer off track in the past, it is never too late to start fresh, right now.

David Hooper

the RICH
SWITCH

The *Simple* 3-Step System To
TURN ON INSTANT WEALTH
Using the Law of Attraction

10-Day Money
Makeover

Simple Steps to Create More Money & Financial Prosperity
Using Emotional Freedom Technique (EFT)

David Hooper

LaVergne, TN USA
03 June 2010
184952LV00001B/21/P